# God's
## Little Princess™
### Devotional
# Bible

Presented to

Presented by

Date

Occasion

General Editor: Sheila Walsh
Gigi, God's Little Princess™ illustrations Copyright © 2005 by Sheila Walsh
Illustrator: Meredith Johnson

Published in Nashville, Tennessee, by Tommy Nelson,®
a Division of Thomas Nelson, Inc.

Typeset and design by: Richmond & Williams, Brentwood, Tennessee
Editorial team: Jennifer Morgan Gerelds, writer;
Beverly Riggs, editor

Printed in China
14 15 16 – 13 12 11

Mfg. by RRD
Shenzhen, China
Jan. 2011/PO #115761

# God's
## Little Princess™
### Devotional
# Bible

## Sheila Walsh

*Scripture selections from the*
International Children's Bible®

THOMAS NELSON
*Since 1798*

For other products and live events,
visit us at: **thomasnelson.com**

# Dear Princess,

*Y*ou hold in your hands stories from the most wonderful book in the world. Within these pages you will discover amazing things you need to know about your Father God and how much he loves you.

Perhaps when you look in the mirror you don't feel like a Princess, but you are a precious daughter of the King of kings.

When I was a little girl I didn't always like being me. I would look at other girls and think that they were prettier than I or smarter than I. Sometimes that made me sad or feel a little lonely, until my mom read these verses to me and helped me to understand how special I am to God:

"You made my whole being.
    You formed me in my mother's body.
I praise you because you made me in an
    amazing and wonderful way.
What you have done is wonderful.
I know this very well."

PSALM 139:13-14

That is great news!

God thinks you are so wonderful, and
he would know, for he made you. I pray that
you will remember, on your good days and
on your not so good days, that God will
never, ever stop loving you.

You are God's little Princess!!

Your big sister,

Sheila

# Introduction for Parents

*E*very girl is a princess, the daughter of a King…the greatest King who created and rules over everything!

Girls long to be beautiful, to be loved, to be adored, to be wanted and needed, and to give their hearts to their hero!

God is that hero. God wants little girls to be all they have the potential to be…to grow up in the warmth and light of his love. The characteristics focused on in this Bible will help young girls blossom into the princesses they were always meant to be. Easy-to-read Scripture selections from the International Children's Bible® are combined with fun and inspiring articles to touch a child's heart. We hope that your little girl will learn about her destiny as a daughter of God and a true princess!

# Features:

**Down In My Heart:** Just like the song says, "I've got the joy, joy, joy, joy down in my heart," these features promote Scripture memory: *"Don't ever forget my words. Keep them deep within your heart."*

PROVERBS 4:21

**Beauty Secrets:** Quick tips on how to be "beautiful"—not just combing your hair, washing your hands, brushing your teeth, and SMILING…

**Bible Princesses:** Girls and women of the Bible who made a difference.

**My Hero:** Scripture promises from God, our ultimate Hero!

**Take a Bow:** Girls love dress-up and role-playing. These articles give tips on how to make quick, easy costumes and put on "plays" that are Bible focused.

**I Adore You!:** Most girls just love singing and dancing. Put that energy to use with kids songs, scriptures, and ways to worship and praise God.

**Princess Charming:** These articles help teach manners, poise and charm…something every princess needs as she graciously says please and thank you to the "subjects" in her kingdom!

**Worthy of Love:** Every princess needs to love not only her family, but also her royal subjects. This feature shows ways to love your parents, siblings, extended family, friends, teachers, and those in the community.

**Royal Truths:** Basic values straight from the Bible, these royal traits are what every princess should possess: honor, charity, fairness, purity, truth, honesty, caring, faithfulness, and many more!

# Table of Contents

# Table of Contents *(continued)*

# Princess Favorites

## Favorite Colors

_____

_____

_____

_____

_____

_____

## Favorite Animals

_____

_____

_____

_____

_____

_____

## Favorite Foods

_____
_____
_____
_____

## Favorite Toys

_____
_____
_____
_____
_____

## Favorite Things to Do

_____
_____
_____
_____

## Favorite Games

_____
_____
_____
_____
_____

## Favorite Songs

_____
_____
_____
_____

## Favorite Bible Verses

_____
_____
_____
_____
_____

God's
Little Princess™
Devotional
Bible

The Lord God said, "It is not good for the man to be alone. I will make a helper who is right for him."

...The man gave names to all the tame animals, to the birds in the sky and to all the wild animals. But Adam did not find a helper that was right for him. So the Lord God caused the man to sleep very deeply. While the man was asleep, God took one of the ribs from the man's body. Then God closed the man's skin at the place where he took the rib. The Lord God used the rib from the man to make a woman. Then the Lord brought the woman to the man.

And the man said, "Now, this is someone whose bones came from my bones. Her body came from my body. I will call her 'woman,' because she was taken out of man."

. . . The man named his wife Eve. This is because she is the mother of everyone who ever lived.

GENESIS 2:18, 20-23; 3:20

*(For more of this story, read Genesis 2:24–3:24.)*

# Eve, Queen of God's World

Imagine what it would be like to be the only girl in the world. Now picture you, God, and Adam—the only boy on the face of the earth. Together, you and Adam are told by God to rule over this incredible creation he has just made.

Eve didn't have to imagine. It really happened to her. She was God's first princess in the Garden of Eden.

It was her job to help Adam take care of the animals, plants, and children that God would one day give them.

Of course, Adam and Eve messed up royally when they listened to Satan instead of God. But God didn't give up on his kids. Instead, he sent his Son Jesus to pay the penalty for sin. Now God's children can reign with Jesus once again.

Now the snake was the most clever of all the wild animals the Lord God had made. One day the snake spoke to the woman. He said, "Did God really say that you must not eat fruit from any tree in the garden?"

... The woman saw that the tree was beautiful. She saw that its fruit was good to eat and that it would make her wise. So she took some of its fruit and ate it. She also gave some of the fruit to her husband who was with her, and he ate it.

Then, it was as if the man's and the woman's eyes were opened. They realized they were naked. So they sewed fig leaves together and made something to cover themselves. . . .

So the Lord God forced the man out of the garden of Eden. He had to work the ground he was taken from. God forced the man out of the garden. Then God put angels on the east side of the garden. He also put a sword of fire there. It flashed around in every direction. This kept people from getting to the tree of life.

GENESIS 3:1, 6-7, 23-24

# Sin Sneaks In

**Take a Bow**

*Directions:* Mom will play both the roles of God and Satan. When speaking for God, mom wears the white scarf; when for the devil, the black scarf. The princess will be Adam and Eve.

* Before play begins, place basket of fruit in the center of the room.

**What you will need:**
- basket of apples or some fruit
- white scarf/cape
- branch with leaves
- black scarf/cape
- coat

**Mom** *(with white scarf)*: "Adam and Eve, I have made you a beautiful garden. Everything in it is yours. Take care of it. Only do not eat from the tree in the center of the garden." *(Point to the basket of fruit in the center of room.)*

**Princess:** *(Walk around the room. Come closer and closer to the basket.)* "My, what lovely fruit grows here!"

**Mom** *(with black scarf)*: *(Hiss.)* "Did God really say that you must not eat fruit from any tree in the garden?"

**Princess:** "We may eat fruit from the trees in the garden except this one. God said that we shouldn't even touch it or we will die."

**Mom** *(still wearing black scarf)*: "You will not die. God knows that if you eat the fruit from that tree, you will learn about good and evil. Then you will be like God!"

**Princess:** "Oh well, it does look very good." *(Take a bite out of the fruit. Snake hisses and goes away.)* "I'll give some to Adam, too. Oh, no! I've done something bad!" *(Use branch with leaves to cover up.)* "I'd better hide from God."

**Mom** *(with white scarf)*: "Adam and Eve, where are you?"

**Princess:** "Hiding from you."

**Mom** *(still with white scarf)*: "Did you eat from the tree I told you not to? Because you did this each of you must pay for your sin. Now, here are some better clothes for you to put on." *(Hand princess the coat.)* "You must now leave the garden."

**Take a Bow!!**

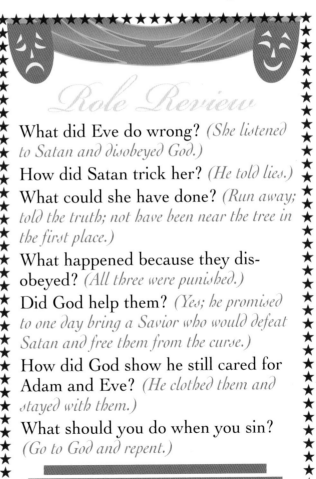

*Role Review*

What did Eve do wrong? *(She listened to Satan and disobeyed God.)*

How did Satan trick her? *(He told lies.)*

What could she have done? *(Run away; told the truth; not have been near the tree in the first place.)*

What happened because they disobeyed? *(All three were punished.)*

Did God help them? *(Yes; he promised to one day bring a Savior who would defeat Satan and free them from the curse.)*

How did God show he still cared for Adam and Eve? *(He clothed them and stayed with them.)*

What should you do when you sin? *(Go to God and repent.)*

When Jared was 162 years old, he had a son named Enoch. After Enoch was born, Jared lived 800 years. During that time he had other sons and daughters. So Jared lived a total of 962 years. Then he died.

When Enoch was 65 years old, he had a son named Methuselah. After Methuselah was born, Enoch walked with God 300 more years. During that time he had other sons and daughters. So Enoch lived a total of 365 years. Enoch walked with God. One day Enoch could not be found, because God took him.

GENESIS 5:18-24

## Royally Loyal

**Royal Truths**

Have you ever visited a nursing home? It's a special place where people who have grown too old to live by themselves go to live. Most of them love to see and visit with young children. It reminds them of when they were once young.

Older people help remind us of some important things, too. They remind us that we won't live on this earth forever. We will grow up, just like they did.

11

At God's right time, we will leave this earth to spend eternity with our King, Jesus. So what will you do with the time God gives you here? God wants us to be loyal to him our whole lives. He wants us to always be his friend and to always trust him to protect and save us.

We don't just belong to God as kids. We need to stay close to him our entire lives until we get to see his face.

Truths

## Make It Yours

In the beginning of time, some people lived close to 1,000 years! Enoch lived 365 years. What's even better is that Enoch became such close friends with God that God took him straight to heaven. Do you want to be loyal to God your whole life like Enoch? Then ask Jesus right now to always keep you close to him. He is able to make it happen!

God said to Abraham, "I will change the name of Sarai, your wife. Her new name will be Sarah. I will bless her. I will give her a son, and you will be the father. She will be the mother of many nations. Kings of nations will come from her."

Abraham bowed facedown on the ground and laughed. He said to himself, "Can a man have a child when he is 100 years old? Can Sarah give birth to a child when she is 90?" Then Abraham said to God, "Please let Ishmael be the son you promised."

God said, "No. Sarah your wife will have a son, and you will name him Isaac. I will make my agreement with him. It will be an agreement that continues forever with all his descendants. . . .

And Sarah said, "God has made me laugh. Everyone who hears about this will laugh with me. No one thought that I would be able to have Abraham's child. But I have given Abraham a son while he is old."

GENESIS 17:15-19; 21:6-7

*(For more of this story, read Genesis 17:1-19; 21:1-12.)*

# Sarah's Crowning Glory

**Bible Princesses**

*S*arah had a different name at first. She was called Sarai when she first met and married Abraham. But then God said he had different plans for both of them. God changed Sarai's name to Sarah, which means "princess." God made a promise to Abraham that he was going to bless him with more descendants than he could count. They were to become the parents of all the Israelites.

*Princesses*

Sarah did have to wait for God, though. She had to wait a really, really long time. She was in her 90's before she had a son, Isaac. Sarah finally understood that God has the power to turn ordinary girls into princesses. She also discovered that God always keeps his promises.

The men asked Abraham, "Where is your wife Sarah?"

"There, in the tent," said Abraham.

Then the Lord said, "I will certainly return to you about this time a year from now. At that time your wife Sarah will have a son."

Sarah was listening at the entrance of the tent which was behind him. Abraham and Sarah were very old. Sarah was past the age when women normally have children. So she laughed to herself, "My husband and I are too old to have a baby."

Then the Lord said to Abraham, "Why did Sarah laugh? Why did she say, 'I am too old to have a baby'? Is there anything too hard for the Lord? No! I will return to you at the right time a year from now. And Sarah will have a son."

GENESIS 18:9-14

*Be full of joy in the Lord always.*
*I will say again, be full of joy.*

PHILIPPIANS 4:4

## Lovely Laugh Lines

**Beauty Secrets**

You can put on a beautiful dress. Color your cheeks with the prettiest pink. Decorate your hair with sparkles and glitter. But if your heart is sad, your real beauty just won't show up.

Sometimes we are sad because hurtful or hard times have come our way.

God promises to comfort us when we cry. But many times, we have a bad look on our face because we have a bad attitude in our heart. Did you not get your way? Did your sister or brother bother you? God says that we should always rejoice in him, no matter what. We can always find a reason to have joy when we remember that he loves and takes care of us.

*Beauty*

Look in the mirror. Make a mad face. Now make a happy face. Which looks better? Which feels better? Ask God to help you always find joy in his friendship. Ask him to help his love put beautiful laugh lines on your face.

Abraham's oldest servant was in charge of everything Abraham owned. Abraham called that servant to him and said, "... Go back to my country, to the land of my relatives. Get a wife for my son Isaac from there."

... The servant said, "Lord, you are the God of my master Abraham. Allow me to find a wife for his son today. Please show this kindness to my master Abraham."

... Before the servant had finished praying, Rebekah came out of the city. She was the daughter of Bethuel. (Bethuel was the son of Milcah and Nahor, Abraham's brother.) Rebekah was carrying her water jar on her shoulder. ...

The servant bowed and worshiped the Lord. He said, "Blessed is the Lord, the God of my master Abraham. The Lord has been kind and truthful to him. He has led me to my master's relatives."

Then Rebekah ran and told her mother's family about all these things. . . .

Laban and Bethuel answered, "This is clearly from the Lord. We cannot change what must happen. Rebekah is yours. Take her and go. Let her marry your master's son as the Lord has commanded."

GENESIS 24:2-4, 12, 15, 26-28, 50-51

*(For more of this story, read all of Genesis 24.)*

# Rebekah, Chosen Royalty

**Bible Princesses**

Rebekah didn't know what was coming. She was just going out to the well to get water, like she did every day. She didn't know that God was watching. God was planning her future. By watering a stranger's camels, she was chosen for a new royal position. God picked her to become Isaac's princess bride. She would become the mother of Jacob. Jacob became the father of Israel, God's chosen people.

Princesses

*D*o you like cleaning your room? Washing dishes? Doing chores around the house? It's easy to get bored and quit. But God is watching. He is training you for your special calling one day. God uses the ordinary things—like watering camels (or feeding your hamster) and serving others—to do mighty works. Like Rebekah, we need to be busy loving Jesus by serving others. God will move at just the right time to work out his amazing plan for your life.

Moses said to the people, "Don't be afraid. God has come to test you. He wants you to respect him so you will not sin."

The people stood far away from the mountain while Moses went near the dark cloud where God was. Then the Lord told Moses to say these things to the Israelites: "You yourselves have seen that I talked with you from heaven. You must not use gold or silver to make idols for yourselves. You must not worship these false gods in addition to me.

"Make an altar of dirt for me. Offer your whole burnt offerings and fellowship offerings on this altar as a sacrifice to me. Use your sheep and your cattle to do this. Worship me in every place that I choose. Then I will come and bless you."

EXODUS 20:20-24

# On Your Honor

**Royal Truths**

*I*f you had a chance to meet the President of the United States, what would you say? Would you be silly? Would you show him respect? Chances are, you would be thrilled! You would give him your complete attention and enjoy every moment.

How much more important than a person is God? We know in our heads that God deserves respect and honor. But in our daily actions we often forget. We might joke about God's Word.

We might think or do other things during family prayer time. We begin to treat God like he is just another person instead of the King of kings.

God does love us. He is our Father, and we can always come to him. But he is also very powerful and holy. He deserves all of our attention, respect, and praise.

Truths

## Make It Yours

In Old Testament days, the Israelites understood God's holiness. His glory amazed them so much that they were afraid to come near the mountain where God spoke to them. Today, we don't need to be afraid of God. Jesus' work on the cross makes us friends and family with him. But we need to remember how important he is. We need to always honor his name. What are some ways you can better show him honor?

Moses cut two stone tablets like the first ones. Then early the next morning he went up to Mount Sinai. He did this just as the Lord had commanded him. Moses carried the two stone tablets with him. Then the Lord came down in the cloud and stood there with Moses. And the Lord called out his name, the Lord.

The Lord passed in front of Moses and said, "I am the Lord. The Lord is a God who shows mercy and is kind. The Lord doesn't become angry quickly. The Lord has great love and faithfulness. The Lord is kind to thousands of people. The Lord forgives people for wrong and sin and turning against him."

EXODUS 34:4-7

# The Gift That Keeps Giving

*Worthy of Love*

All year long you wait. Is anything more exciting than Christmas day? People all around the world celebrate by getting together, giving fun gifts, and eating good food. God's people enjoy it most because we know Jesus, God's greatest gift of all.

Have you ever wondered why such a great day happens only once a year? What keeps us from celebrating Jesus every single day?

31

*D*on't wait any longer. Look for ways that you can surprise your family with little gifts of love each day. Sneak a picture onto your mom's pillow at night. Play a special game with your little sister. Tell your older brother how much you love him. Tell your daddy "thank you" for working so hard for the family.

Gifts don't have to be big. They just need to come from your heart.

$\mathcal{E}$ach day is a new chance for you to celebrate God's love by showing it to others. It will remind your family that God's goodness lasts all year—and all of our lives!

There was a prophetess named Deborah. She was the wife of Lappidoth. She was judge of Israel at that time. Deborah would sit under the Palm Tree of Deborah. This was between the cities of Ramah and Bethel, in the mountains of Ephraim. And the people of Israel would come to her to settle their arguments.

Deborah sent a message to a man named Barak. He was the son of Abinoam. Barak lived in the city of Kedesh, which is in the area of Naphtali. Deborah said to Barak, "The Lord, the God of Israel, commands you: 'Go and gather 10,000

men of Naphtali and Zebulun.
Lead them to Mount Tabor. . . .'"

Then Barak said to Deborah,
"I will go if you will go with me.
But if you will not go with me,
I won't go."

"Of course I will go with you,"
Deborah answered. "But you will not
get credit for the victory. The Lord
will let a woman defeat Sisera." So
Deborah went with Barak to Kedesh.

JUDGES 4:4-6, 8-9

*Judges*

# A Sticky Situation

**Princess Charming**

You're in the grocery store with your mom when you spot your favorite candy. You ask if you can have it, but mom says "no." Do you:

**A** Say, "Yes ma'am" and turn your attention to something else.

**B** Yell, "Why not?" or "That's not fair!"

**C** Argue, telling your mom that you think she's mean.

**D** Start crying, groaning, or begging.

The temptation may be to do all of B, C, and D. It's always hard to hear the word "no." We like to get our way, right away. But God says that obeying and honoring our parents is more important than getting what we want. We need to trust God that his way is best. If we want to act like royalty, we must remember to respect what our parents say—no matter what!

Naomi said, "Look, your sister-in-law is going back to her own people and her own gods. Go back with her."

But Ruth said, "Don't ask me to leave you! Don't beg me not to follow you! Every place you go, I will go. Every place you live, I will live. Your people will be my people. Your God will be my God. And where you die, I will die. And there I will be buried. I ask the Lord to punish me terribly if I do not keep this promise: Only death will separate us."

. . . So Naomi and her daughter-in-law Ruth, the woman from Moab, came back from Moab. They came to

Bethlehem at the beginning of the barley harvest. . . .

Then Boaz said, "The Lord bless you, my daughter. Your kindness to me is greater than the kindness you showed to Naomi in the beginning. You didn't look for a young man to marry, either rich or poor. Now, my daughter, don't be afraid. I will do everything you ask. All the people in our town know you are a very good woman."

RUTH 1:15-17, 22; 3:10-11

*(For more of this story, read all 4 chapters of the Book of Ruth.)*

# Ruth, a Secret Royalty

At first glance, Ruth doesn't look much like royalty. She grew up in a country that didn't serve God. Her husband died, and she didn't have any money. So she and her husband's mother, Naomi, went back to Israel where they could be near others who loved God.

God blessed Ruth for her kindness to Naomi. He gave Ruth another husband who loved and worshiped God. Then they all had enough money and food to live on.

Princesses

God also gave them a son who would one day become the grandfather of King David. In time, Jesus was born from her family line.

Ruth reminds us that, even though we might not look very rich or powerful on the outside, we are still royalty. As Christians, we are children of the King!

Once, after they had eaten their meal in Shiloh, Hannah got up. Now Eli the priest was sitting on a chair near the entrance to the Lord's Holy Tent. Hannah was very sad. She cried much and prayed to the Lord. She made a promise. She said, "Lord of heaven's armies, see how bad I feel. Remember me! Don't forget me. If you will give me a son, I will give him back to you all his life. And no one will ever use a razor to cut his hair."

… Eli answered, "Go in peace. May the God of Israel give you what you asked of him."

… So Hannah became pregnant, and in time she gave birth to a son. She named him Samuel. She said, "His name is Samuel because I asked the Lord for him."

1 SAMUEL 1:9-11, 17, 20

# Heaven Hears

Hannah had a problem. She wanted to have a baby. She knew she couldn't make it happen, but God could. So she prayed to God. God heard her prayer and gave her a baby boy.

What do you need for today? Do you need help being kind to your sister or brother? Are you scared to go to school? Do you want help sharing Jesus with others? Do you need help obeying your mom or dad?

God says that he wants us to talk to him about everything! If it's on your mind, tell it to God. You can pray while you're walking, riding in the car, playing outside, or wherever. God promises to listen. Best of all, he knows just what you really need. Even though his answer might not be what you expected, his way is always what is best for us.

Hero

We need to always pray about everything. We should pray during the good times and even when we're going through tough times. This teaches us to trust God. Prayer is an invitation for God to do his amazing work in our lives!

Eli's eyes were so weak he was almost blind. One night he was lying in bed. Samuel was also in bed in the Lord's Holy Tent. The Box of the Agreement was in the Holy Tent. God's lamp was still burning.

Then the Lord called Samuel. Samuel answered, "I am here!" He ran to Eli and said, "I am here. You called me."

But Eli said, "I didn't call you. Go back to bed." So Samuel went back to bed.

The Lord called again, "Samuel!"

Samuel again went to Eli and said, "I am here. You called me."

Again Eli said, "I didn't call you. Go back to bed."

Samuel did not yet know the Lord. The Lord had not spoken directly to him yet.

The Lord called Samuel for the third time. Samuel got up and went to Eli. He said, "I am here. You called me."

Then Eli realized the Lord was calling the boy. So he told Samuel, "Go to bed. If he calls you again, say, 'Speak, Lord. I am your servant, and I am listening.'" So Samuel went and lay down in bed.

The Lord came and stood there. He called as he had before. He said, "Samuel, Samuel!"

Samuel said, "Speak, Lord. I am your servant, and I am listening."

1 SAMUEL 3:2-10

# A Lesson in Listening

Take a Bow

**What you will need:**
- box
- bed
- flashlight or lamp

**Mom:** *(Read opening.)* "The boy Samuel served the Lord under Eli. One night Eli was lying in bed. Samuel was also in bed in the Lord's Holy Tent. The Box of the Agreement was in the Holy Tent. God's lamp was still burning."

**Mom** *(in a deep voice)*: "Samuel! Samuel!"

**Princess:** "I am here! *(Get up and run to Eli.)* I am here. You called me."

**Mom** *(as Eli)*: "I didn't call you. Go back to bed."
*(Samuel returns to bed.)*

**Mom** *(in a deep voice)*: "Samuel! Samuel!"

**Princess** *(runs to Eli again)*: "I am here. You called me!"

**Mom** *(as Eli)*: "I didn't call you. Go back to bed."
*(Samuel returns to bed again.)*

**Mom** *(in a deep voice)*: "Samuel! Samuel!"

**Princess** *(runs to Eli)*: "I am here!! You called me!"

**Mom** *(as Eli)*: "It must be the Lord God who is calling you. If he calls you again, say, 'Speak Lord, I am your servant, and I am listening.'" *(Samuel returns to bed.)*

**Mom** *(in a deep voice)*: "Samuel, Samuel!"

**Princess:** "Speak Lord, I am your servant, and I am listening."

**Mom:** *(Narrate the ending.)* "The Lord was with Samuel as he grew up. He did not let any of Samuel's messages fail to come true. Then all Israel, from Dan to Beersheba, knew Samuel was a prophet."

### Take a Bow!!

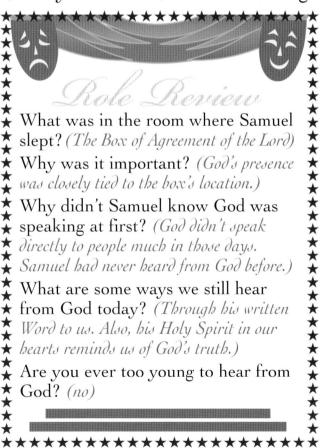

*Role Review*

What was in the room where Samuel slept? *(The Box of Agreement of the Lord)*

Why was it important? *(God's presence was closely tied to the box's location.)*

Why didn't Samuel know God was speaking at first? *(God didn't speak directly to people much in those days. Samuel had never heard from God before.)*

What are some ways we still hear from God today? *(Through his written Word to us. Also, his Holy Spirit in our hearts reminds us of God's truth.)*

Are you ever too young to hear from God? *(no)*

The Lord said to Samuel, ". . . I am sending you to Jesse who lives in Bethlehem. I have chosen one of his sons to be king."

. . . When they arrived, Samuel saw Eliab. Samuel thought, "Surely the Lord has appointed this person standing here before him."

But the Lord said to Samuel, ". . . God does not see the same way people see. People look at the outside of a person, but the Lord looks at the heart."

. . . So Samuel took the container of olive oil. Then he poured oil on Jesse's youngest son to appoint him in front of his brothers. From that day on, the Lord's Spirit entered David with power.

1 SAMUEL 16:1, 6-7, 13

## Life Through God's Glasses

**Beauty Secrets**

Do you have to wear glasses to see well? Do you know someone who does? Glasses help our eyes to see more clearly what is in front of us. In many ways, the Bible acts like glasses for God's children. It helps us to see God's truth in the world around us.

People who don't know God will not be able to see life the way we do. God wants us to see other people through his glasses. We don't need to look at their clothes, hair, or shape to see if they matter. Other people are important because God loves them—and so should we.

# Beauty

# Beauty Tips

Do you (or your mom) have a pair of sunglasses? Try them on. How does what you see look different? Ask God to help you see his world the way he does. Ask him to help you love others for who they are on the inside, not what you see on the outside.

Elijah stood before the people. He said, "How long will you try to serve both Baal and the Lord? If the Lord is the true God, follow him. But if Baal is the true God, follow him!"

But the people said nothing. . . .

Then Elijah said to the prophets of Baal, "There are many of you. So you go first. Choose a bull and prepare it. Pray to your god, but don't start the fire."

So they took the bull that was given to them and prepared it. They prayed to Baal from morning until noon. They shouted, "Baal, answer us!" But there was no sound. No one answered. . . .

Then Elijah said to all the people, "Now come to me." So they gathered around him. Elijah rebuilt the altar of the Lord because it had been torn down. . . .

It was time for the evening sacrifice. So the prophet Elijah went near the altar. He prayed, "Lord, you are the God of Abraham, Isaac and Israel. I ask you now to prove that you are the God of Israel. And prove that I am your servant. Show these people that you commanded me to do all these things. Lord, answer my prayer. Show these people that you, Lord, are God. Then the people will know that you are bringing them back to you."

Then fire from the Lord came down. It burned the sacrifice, the wood, the stones and the ground around the altar. It also dried up the water in the ditch.

1 KINGS 18:21, 25-26, 30, 36-38

# My Daddy's Bigger

Imagine going camping with your family. Dad tells you to gather sticks for the campfire. After you put them in a pile, your dad pours water all over them! Then he calls out to God to make the fire start. Sound crazy?

It's similar to what God had Elijah, his prophet, do. God wanted to prove that he alone is God and that all the people who worshiped false idols were wrong. When the people saw God's work, they forgot Baal and followed God again.

God still wants people to know he rules all things. Many other people in this world do not know our God. Like Baal's prophets, they may try to get us to believe lies.

We need to remember that God is our King. He alone has all the power. We can boldly tell others how great God is. Nothing can defeat our heavenly Father. He's the King of all creation!

Hero

The wife of a man from a group of the prophets came to Elisha. She said, "Your servant, my husband, is dead! You know he honored the Lord. But now the man he owes money to is coming to take my two boys. He will make them his slaves!"

Elisha answered, "How can I help you? Tell me, what do you have in your house?"

The woman said, "I don't have anything there except a pot of oil."

Then Elisha said, "Go and get empty jars from all your neighbors. Don't ask for just a few. Then you must go into your house and close the door. Only you and your sons will be there. Then pour oil into all the jars. Set the full ones to one side."

She left Elisha and shut the door. Only she and her sons were in the house. As they brought the jars to her, she poured the oil. When the jars were all full, she said to her son, "Bring me another jar."

But he said, "There are no more jars." Then the oil stopped flowing.

She went and told Elisha. Elisha said to her, "Go. Sell the oil and pay what you owe. You and your sons can live on what is left."

2 KINGS 4:1-7

# Oil of Gladness

Take a Bow

*Directions: Mom will be Elisha. Princess will play the part of the widow. Any other siblings can be the sons, or you can use dolls in their place. Place cups around the room for princess to gather later. Fill pitcher with water and place on a table near the center of the room.*

**What you will need:**
- pitcher filled with water
- several cups or bowls
- shawl for widow
- cape or cloak for Elisha

**Princess** *(wearing widow's shawl, walks up to Elisha)*: "Your servant, my husband, is dead! You know he honored the Lord. But now the man he owes money to is coming to take my two boys. He will make them his slaves!"

**Mom** *(wearing cloak as Elisha)*: "How can I help you? Tell me, what do you have in your house?"

**Princess**: "I don't have anything there except a pot of oil *(point to the pitcher of water)*.

**Mom**: "Go and get empty jars from all your neighbors. Don't ask for just a few. Then you must go into your house and close the door. Only you and your sons will be there. Then pour oil into all the jars. Set the full ones to one side."

**Princess**: *(Walk around the room and gather the cups placed there. Pretend to knock on neighbors' doors asking for any more jars. Then come to the table. Pour water into each of the cups.)*

"There aren't any more jars to fill. This one pot of oil has filled every-thing I have!"

**Mom**: "Very well! Go now. Sell the oil, and pay what you owe. You and your sons can live on what is left."

***Take a Bow!!***

*Role Review*

Why was the widow upset? *(Her husband was dead, she had no money, and her sons were going to be sold as slaves.)*

Why did Elisha tell her to get jars from her neighbors? *(to hold the oil)*

How was she able to fill so many jars from one pot of oil? *(It was a miracle from God.)*

How did the oil help her and her sons? *(She could sell it and get money to live on.)*

If you have a need, what should you do? *(Like the widow, ask God for help and trust him to provide.)*

Naaman was commander of the army of the king of Aram. He was a great man to his master. He had much honor because the Lord had used him to give victory to Aram. He was a mighty and brave man. But he had a harmful skin disease.

The Arameans had gone out to steal from the Israelites. And they had taken a little girl as a captive from Israel. This little girl served Naaman's wife. She said to her mistress, "I wish that my master would meet the prophet who lives in Samaria. He would heal Naaman of his disease."

Naaman went to the king. He told him what the girl from Israel had said....

The king of Israel read the letter. Then he tore his clothes to show how upset he was. He said, "I'm not God! I can't kill and make alive again! Why does this man send someone with a harmful skin disease for me to heal? You can see that the king of Aram is trying to start trouble with me!"

...So Naaman went with his horses and chariots to Elisha's house. And he stood outside the door.

Elisha sent a messenger to Naaman. The messenger said, "Go and wash in the Jordan River seven times. Then your skin will be healed, and you will be clean."

...So Naaman went down and dipped in the Jordan seven times. He did just as Elisha had said. Then Naaman's skin became new again. It was like the skin of a little boy. And Naaman was clean!

Naaman and all his group came back to Elisha. He stood before Elisha and said, "Look. I now know there is no God in all the earth except in Israel! Now please accept a gift from me."

2 KINGS 5:1-4, 7, 9-10, 14-15

# From Rags to True Riches

Take a Bow

*Directions:* Scene begins with Naaman's servant girl (the princess) and his wife (mom). Then roles switch to Naaman (played by the princess), the king of Israel, and Elisha (both played by mom).

**What you will need:**
- toilet paper
- crown
- scarf or hood

**Mom** *(as Naaman's wife speaking to servant girl)*: "Naaman is such a good man. He is the commander of the king's army. He has won so many battles and fought so bravely. But he cannot fight this terrible skin disease!"

**Princess:** "Ma'am, I have an idea. There is a prophet who lives in Samaria. He can heal your husband of this disease! His name is Elisha."

**Mom:** "I will tell him right away!"
*(Scene closes. Roles change.)*

**Princess** *(in rags)*: "I have 750 pounds of silver and 150 pounds of gold. Surely Israel's king will help me."
*(Walk up to mom wearing the crown.)*
"Hear, O king of Israel. This letter is from my king of Aram. He asks that you heal me from my skin disease."

*Directions:* Use the toilet paper to wrap princess's arms, legs, and body in mummy style. As the king of Israel, mom wears the crown. When speaking as Elisha, remove crown and wear the scarf or hood.

**Mom** *(as king)*: *(Throw off your hood and act distressed.)* "What? I'm not God! I can't kill and make alive again! The king of Aram must be trying to start a war with me! Look, Elisha has sent me a letter. He says that he can help you. Go to him!"

**Princess:** *(Walk to door or table, and knock.)* "Elisha, Elisha! I've come to you for help!"

**Mom** *(as Elisha, wearing hood)*: "Go wash yourself in the Jordan River seven times and you will be clean."

**Princess:** *(Pretend to dip seven times in the river. Take off the toilet paper.)* "Look! My skin is like a young boy's! I've been healed. Now I know there is no God in all the earth except in Israel!"

**Take a Bow!!**

## Role Review

What was Naaman's problem? *(He had a skin disease that no one could cure.)*

Who told him about Elisha? *(Naaman's young servant girl from Israel)*

Was Israel's king powerful enough to help Naaman? *(no)*

Who did help Naaman? *(Elisha)*

How? *(He washed himself seven times in the Jordan River.)*

Can you really wash off a skin disease? *(no)*

Who really healed Naaman? *(God)*

The king's personal servants had a suggestion. They said, "Let a search be made for beautiful young virgins for the king."

. . . Mordecai had a cousin named Hadassah, who had no father or mother. So Mordecai took care of her. Hadassah was also called Esther, and she had a very pretty figure and face. Mordecai had adopted her as his own daughter when her father and mother died.

The king's command and order had been heard. And many girls had been brought to the palace in Susa. They had been put under the care of Hegai. When this happened, Esther was also taken to the king's palace. She was put into the care of Hegai, who was in charge of the women. Esther pleased Hegai, and he liked her. So Hegai quickly began giving Esther her beauty treatments and special food. He gave her seven servant girls chosen from the king's palace. Then Hegai moved Esther and her seven servant girls to the best part of the women's quarters. . . .

And the king was pleased with Esther more than with any of the other virgins. And he liked her more than any of the others. So King Xerxes put a royal crown on Esther's head. And he made her queen in place of Vashti.

ESTHER 2:2, 7-9, 17

*(For more of this story, read the first 8 chapters of the Book of Esther.)*

# Esther, Beautiful on the Inside and Out

Esther wasn't supposed to be important. Both of her parents had died. As an orphan, she was raised by her cousin, Mordecai. They were both Jews who lived in the foreign land of Persia. Persia's king didn't know God.

But God knew Esther. He had something special in store for her. Persia's king chose Esther to be queen over all the other women in the kingdom. Esther didn't become proud or forget her people.

Princesses

$\mathcal{I}$nstead, she used her position to help save all the Jews from a wicked man named Haman. Haman wanted to kill God's people so he could have more power. Esther trusted God to protect her. In the end, Haman was killed, and God's people lived in peace.

Do you ever feel unloved or ordinary? Remember that God sees you, too. Because he loves you, you can be brave like Esther and obey whatever God says. Trust Jesus as he shows you your special place in his world.

Esther sent this answer to Mordecai: "Go and get all the Jews in Susa together. For my sake, give up eating. Do not eat or drink for three days, night and day. I and my servant girls will also give up eating. Then I will go to the king, even though it is against the law. And if I die, I die."

So Mordecai went away. He did everything Esther had told him to do.

On the third day Esther put on her royal robes. Then she stood in the inner courtyard of the king's palace, facing the king's hall. The king was sitting on his royal throne in the hall, facing the doorway. The king saw Queen Esther standing in the court-yard. When he saw her, he was very pleased. He held out to her the gold scepter that was in his hand. So Esther went up to him and touched the end of the scepter.

ESTHER 4:15–5:2

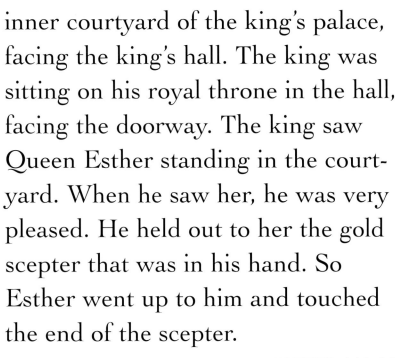

# The Perfect Excuse

**Princess Charming**

You've finished eating. Still seated at the table, you notice your parents are busy talking. Should you:

**A** Get up and leave.

**B** Interrupt their conversation, and tell them you're finished.

**C** Wait until they stop talking. Then say, "Excuse me," and ask for permission to get up.

If you answered C, you truly are a princess-in-waiting. It's always polite to let others go first before you begin talking. It's even better to say "excuse me" when you do need to speak up and say something to grown-ups. Saying "excuse me" also works wonders if you burp, sneeze, or just need to get somewhere without knocking someone over!

My heart is right, God.
My heart is right.
I will sing and praise you.

Wake up, my soul.
Wake up, harp and lyre!
I will wake up the dawn.

Lord, I will praise you among the nations.
I will sing songs of praise about you to
all the nations.

Your love is so great it reaches to
the skies.
Your truth reaches to the clouds.

God, you are supreme over the skies.
Let your glory be over all the earth.

PSALM 57:7-11

74

## Rise and Shine

*I Adore You!*

What's the first thing you do when you wake up in the morning? Do you hop out of bed and go to the bathroom? Brush your teeth? Play? Climb in bed with mom and dad? Each day is new. Each day is another chance to discover all the fun blessings God has waiting for you.

But the very best part happens before you even get out of bed, while you're still snuggled under your covers.

When all is still quiet, when the light is just streaming in your window, you can talk to God. You can think about his goodness. Remember his love for you. You can thank him for watching over you through the night. Then give him the day that lies ahead. Ask him to guide you through it.

Adore

*L*ike the birds outside your window, you can sing your praise and thankfulness to him. It's the best beginning to a beautiful day in Jesus. You can hum a happy tune while you are brushing your teeth.

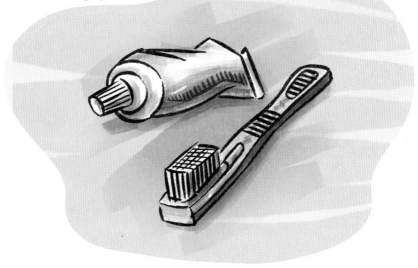

God, you are my God.
I want to follow you.
My whole being thirsts for you,
like a man in a dry, empty land
where there is no water.

I have seen you in the Temple.
I have seen your strength and glory.

Your love is better than life.
I will praise you.

I will praise you as long as I live.
I will lift up my hands in prayer
   to your name.

I will be content as if I had eaten
   the best foods.
My lips will sing. My mouth will
   praise you.

PSALM 63:1-5

## Signs of Life

*I Adore You!*

Did you know that not everyone can sing with their voices? People who are deaf cannot hear music. They can't even hear themselves when they talk or sing. So they talk and sing in a different and exciting way—with their hands!

Hand motions to music can help us feel and understand the words even better, too. Using our hands and arms can help us express the joy and excitement that is in our hearts.

Whether we can hear with our ears or sing well with our voices, God wants us to praise him with everything we have in us. How many different ways can you think of to worship?

## Activity

Using the song *Jesus Loves Me*, create your own hand motions that help show the words of the song. Then sing it to the Lord, using your mouth and your hands!

# Jesus Loves Me

ANNA B. WARNER

Jesus loves me, this I know,

For the Bible tells me so;

Little ones to Him belong;

They are weak, but He is strong.

Yes, Jesus loves me!

Yes, Jesus loves me!

Yes, Jesus loves me!

The Bible tells me so.

The Lord is your protection.
You have made God Most High
your place of safety.

Nothing bad will happen to you.
No disaster will come to your home.

He has put his angels in charge
of you.
They will watch over you wherever
you go.

They will catch you with their hands.
And you will not hit your foot
on a rock.

PSALM 91:9-12

# Heavenly Help

Did you know that angels are real? That's right! God made special beings that we normally can't see with our eyes. He made them even before he made people. They serve God and worship him in heaven.

*Down In My Heart*

## Memory Portion:

He has put his angels in charge of you. They will watch over you wherever you go.

PSALM 91:11

When God made us, he gave his angels another special job. He told them to protect and take care of his royal children! So have fun working, playing, and even sleeping. God and his angels are watching and guiding you. You are never alone, and you never have to be afraid.

# All Night, All Day

WRITER UNKNOWN

All night, all day, angels watchin'
  over me, my Lord.
All night, all day, angels watchin'
  over me.

Sun is a-settin' in the West;
  angels watchin' over me.
Sleep, my child, take your rest;
  angels watchin' over me.

All night, all day, angels watchin'
  over me, my Lord.
All night, all day, angels watchin'
  over me.

My whole being, praise the Lord.
Lord my God, you are very great.
You are clothed with glory and majesty.

You wear light like a robe.
You stretch out the skies like a tent.

You build your room above the clouds.
You make the clouds your chariot.
You ride on the wings of the wind.

You make the winds your messengers.
Flames of fire are your servants. . . .

Lord, you have made many things.
With your wisdom you made them all.
The earth is full of your riches.

PSALM 104:1-4, 24

## Heaven on Earth

Have you ever wondered what heaven will be like? God gives us little glimpses all around us in the world he has made. Look at the stars. Can you even count them? Look at the mountains. Could any person make anything so big and grand? Look at the ocean full of amazing creatures. Look at the sunset and all of its beautiful colors. Is anyone more creative than God?

God's creation shouts out how incredible he is. When we see the tiniest flower bloom or the largest summer thunderstorm, we need to remember the One who made it all. Think of how spectacular his creation is. Then tell God the Creator how wonderful you think he is for making it like he did.

Adore

# This Is My Father's World

### MALTBIE D. BABCOCK

This is my Father's world,
And to my listening ears,
All nature sings, and 'round me rings
The music of the spheres.
This is my Father's world!
I rest me in the thought,
Of rocks and trees, of skies and seas—
His hand the wonders wrought.

Happy are the people who
　　live pure lives.
They follow the Lord's teachings.

Happy are the people who keep his rules.
They ask him for help with their
　　whole heart. . . .

How can a young person live a pure life?
He can do it by obeying your word.

With all my heart I try to obey you, God.
Don't let me break your commands.

I have taken your words to heart
so I would not sin against you.

Lord, you should be praised.
Teach me your demands.

PSALM 119:1-2, 9-12

# God's Hidden Treasure

The Bible has a lot of words in it. In fact, it is probably longer than any other book on your shelf. So how can a royal princess possibly remember all the words her heavenly Father has told her?

*Memory Portion:*

How can a young person live a pure life? He can do it by obeying your word.

PSALM 119:9

*R*emember that God put his Spirit inside your heart to help you learn his ways. Ask the Holy Spirit to help you. Then, when you hear a special verse that helps you know God better, tell your parents about it. Read it each day when you wake up, at meals, in the car, or whenever you think about it. Soon God's Word will be hiding in your heart like a treasure, and you'll never forget it!

*Heart*

# I've Got the Joy, Joy, Joy, Joy Down in My Heart

WRITER UNKNOWN

I've got the joy, joy, joy,
joy down in my heart.
Down in my heart; down in my heart.
I've got the joy, joy, joy,
joy down in my heart.
Down in my heart to stay.

I've got the love of Jesus,
love of Jesus down in my heart.
Down in my heart; down in my heart.
I've got the love of Jesus,
love of Jesus down in my heart.
Down in my heart to stay.

You made my whole being.
You formed me in my
mother's body.

I praise you because you made me
in an amazing and wonderful way.
What you have done is wonderful.
I know this very well.

You saw my bones being formed
as I took shape in my mother's body.
When I was put together there,
you saw my body as it was formed.
All the days planned for me
were written in your book
before I was one day old.

PSALM 139:13-16

# Fashioned and Fabulous

**Down In My Heart**

When you look in the mirror, do you like what you see? God sure does! In fact, God has been planning you for a very long time. Even before he made the earth, God knew exactly when and how he would make you.

*Memory Portion:*

I praise you because you made me in
an amazing and wonderful way.
What you have done is wonderful.
I know this very well.

PSALM 139:14

God makes each of his children very different so that we can bring him glory in our own special way. Are your eyes brown or blue? Is your hair long or short? Is your skin smooth or freckly? Thank God right now for the creative and beautiful way he made you. Then ask him to help you use your gifts to bless others and glorify him.

*Heart*

# Activity

What is it about you that makes you special? Why do you think God made you that way? Ask your mom to help you make a list of your special traits to remind you how God has blessed you. Take time now to thank him for making you like you are for his special plan. Ask him to show you how to use your gifts to bless others.

Praise him with trumpet blasts.
   Praise him with harps and lyres.

Praise him with tambourines
   and dancing.
Praise him with stringed instruments
   and flutes.

Praise him with loud cymbals.
Praise him with crashing cymbals.

Let everything that breathes praise
   the Lord.

Praise the Lord!

PSALM 150:3-6

## Joyful Noise

I Adore You!

Take time to visit the outdoors. Do you see the big blue sky? Can you hear the birds and crickets chirping in the wind? God has made it all. Everything he has made was designed to bring him praise.

What about you? Are you ready to praise the Lord? All you need is a loud voice and a little creativity.

Do you have some kitchen items, like a wooden spoon and a big pot lid? How about some rice to put into a jar with a lid? Take a look around you in the room. Can you spot any other potential noisemakers? Then grab it and let's go!

God says he wants us to declare his praise—and he doesn't want us to be quiet about it, either.

*Adore*

Use your new-found instruments to make a joyful noise to the Lord. March around the room, singing your favorite praise song or thanking God out loud for how great he is. You can even put on a praise music CD or tape to help. Don't forget to play your instruments!

"Wisdom is the most important
     thing. So get wisdom.
If it costs everything you have,
   get understanding.

Believe in the value of wisdom,
   and it will make you great.
Use it, and it will bring honor to you.

Like flowers in your hair,
   it will beautify your life.
Like a crown, it will make you
   look beautiful."

My child, listen and accept what I say.
Then you will have a long life.

PROVERBS 4:7-10

102

# Women of Wisdom

**Royal Truths**

Solomon had his chance. God said that he would give him anything he wanted. Can you imagine? What would you ask for if you could have anything in the world?

Solomon had just become king in place of his father, David. More than anything else, he wanted to be a wise ruler. So he asked God for wisdom. God was more than pleased to grant his wish. He made him the wisest man in the world and added fame and wealth, too!

God says that we need to want to be wise, too. Where does wisdom come from? It comes from God! He helps our weak minds understand how great God is. The more we understand about God, the wiser we become.

Our wisdom changes our thoughts, actions, and lives. We make better choices that please God. We begin to think more like him.

Then we are able to help others know God better, too. God-given wisdom is our crown of beauty that leads us and others to him.

Truths

## Make It Yours

How can you get a better understanding of God? In James 1:5, God says all you have to do is ask! God actually loves to give us the gift of wisdom. He wants you to know him better and understand his ways. Take time right now to ask God to make you wise like Solomon. Remember to study his Word so you will grow in his truth.

Go watch the ants, you lazy person.
Watch what they do and be wise.
Ants have no commander.
They have no leader or ruler.
But they store up food in the summer.
They gather their supplies at harvest.
How long will you lie there,
  you lazy person?
When will you get up from sleeping?
You sleep a little; you take a nap.
You fold your hands and rest.
So you will be as poor as if you had
  been robbed.
You will have as little as if you had
  been held up.

PROVERBS 6:6-11

# Crawling with Wisdom

**Worthy of Love**

Solomon doesn't want you to get bitten! He just wants you to get better... better at doing the work that needs to be done. He tells us in Proverbs to go watch the ants. Do they ever stop working? Is their job easy? Do they ever complain?

Truth is, they don't even need to be told what to do. They know what their job is, and they just do it.

So how about you? Do you know what work needs to be done around the house? Do you know to take up your dishes after you've finished? Do you know to put up your toys when you're finished playing? Do you do it on your own, or do you wait until mom or dad makes you do it?

Make today your first ant day. Look around the house for ways to help your mom clean, beginning with your own mess. Make up your bed. Pick up your toys.

*Love*

*T*hen ask your mom if you can dust or help her in some other way. Working without being asked is a sure sign you are growing up. It also shows God's love in your heart as you work to serve others. You will become wise like the ant, and a wonderful help to your home!

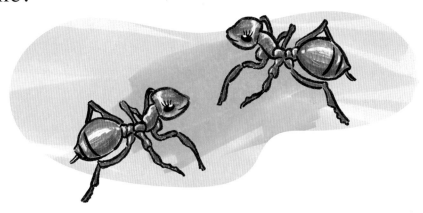

It is hard to find an excellent wife.
She is worth more than rubies.

Her husband trusts her completely.
With her, he has everything he needs....

She speaks wise words.
And she teaches others to be kind.

She watches over her family.
And she is always busy.

Her children bless her.
Her husband also praises her....

Charm can fool you,
   and beauty can trick you.
But a woman who respects the Lord
   should be praised.

PROVERBS 31:10-11, 26-28, 30

*It is hard to find an excellent wife.*
*She is worth more than rubies.*

PROVERBS 31:10

## You Are a Jewel

**Beauty Secrets** Did you know that you are a princess-in-training? You won't be a little girl forever. You are growing taller, older, and smarter each day. Are you hiding God's Word in your heart? Then you are also growing more like Jesus, too.

One day, God may allow you to grow up and get married. You will be the queen of the house. You will have your own little ones to love. So how can you be a good wife and mom? Start practicing now. Learn to love and serve others. Use your time wisely. Work with your mom to see how she does it. Most importantly, ask Jesus for help. If you do, he says that you will be even more beautiful than precious jewels.

*Beauty*

*Beauty Tips*

Pick out your favorite beaded necklace from your dress-up clothes. (Or you can choose a ring.) Put it on. When you touch it or see it during the day, remember that you are God's precious jewel. Then ask God to help you grow up to become the special woman he wants you to be.

There is a right time for everything.
Everything on earth has its
special season.

There is a time to be born
and a time to die.

There is a time to plant
and a time to pull up plants.

There is a time to kill
and a time to heal.

There is a time to destroy
and a time to build.

There is a time to cry
and a time to laugh.

There is a time to be sad
and a time to dance.

There is a time to throw away stones
and a time to gather them.

There is a time to hug
and a time not to hug.

There is a time to look for something
and a time to stop looking for it.

There is a time to keep things
and a time to throw things away.

There is a time to tear apart
and a time to sew together.

There is a time to be silent
and a time to speak.

There is a time to love
and a time to hate.

There is a time for war
and a time for peace.

ECCLESIASTES 3:1-8

*Ecclesiastes*

# Hold Your Horses

**Princess Charming**

Sunday school is over, and it is time to go to "big church" with your mom and dad. After a few minutes of sitting, you want to do something else. The preacher is talking, and everyone else is quiet. You decide to:

**A** Ask your parents, "When is it going to be over?" again and again.

**B** Slide out of your chair, and bump the people in front of you.

**C** Start fighting with your brothers and sisters.

**D** Sit quietly and listen. Talk to God in your heart about whatever is on your mind.

"Why do I have to just sit here when I could be doing something else?" you might want to yell. And it's not just at church. Sometimes you have to be still at restaurants or at other people's houses. Sitting still and being quiet is not a lot of fun. But every good princess knows that there is a perfect time for everything. There is a time for fun and a time to sit still. Be patient. Listen to what is going on around you. You might learn something new! The time for fun and playing is just around the corner.

117

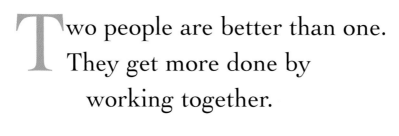

Two people are better than one.
    They get more done by
        working together.

If one person falls,
    the other can help him up.
But it is bad for the person who
    is alone when he falls.
No one is there to help him.

If two lie down together,
    they will be warm.
But a person alone will
    not be warm.

An enemy might defeat one person,
but two people together can
defend themselves.
A rope that has three parts wrapped
together is hard to break.

ECCLESIASTES 4:9-12

# Fun with Friends

**Princess Charming**

You are playing with one of your favorite friends. Suddenly, someone new walks over and asks if they can play, too. You decide to:

**A** Tell the girl to go away; you are busy.

**B** Tell her there's not enough room for all of you.

**C** Invite her to join in the fun.

**D** Tell her no; she's not your friend.

Everyone loves to spend time with friends. After all, friends are a big gift from our heavenly King. However, God wants us to love and be kind to everyone, not just our friends. He wants us to be a friend to others who are lonely. When we show kindness to others, it helps them feel the love of Jesus through us. It's also a great way to get to know them better. Soon you'll have lots of friends. Playtime will be better than ever!

"My darling, everything about
you is beautiful.
There is nothing at all
wrong with you.

Come with me from Lebanon,
my bride.
Come with me from Lebanon.
Come from the top of Mount Amana,
from the tops of Mount Senir
and Mount Hermon.
Come from the lions' dens
and from the leopards' hills.

My sister, my bride,
   you have thrilled my heart.
You have thrilled my heart
   with a glance of your eyes,
   with one jewel from
      your necklace.

Your love is so sweet, my sister,
      my bride!
   Your love is better than wine.
   Your perfume smells better
      than any spice."

SONG OF SONGS 4:7-10

# The King's Beautiful Bride

In every good princess story, a prince charming stands ready to take his bride. King Solomon found his fairy-tale princess. She was a woman from the city of Shulam. Though he never gives her name, he tells us a lot about how beautiful and wonderful she is.

Why was the Shulamite woman so special? She loved Solomon with her whole heart. More than anything, she loved to be with him. All of her friends could see that they were perfect for each other.

Princesses

In the end, the king married his beautiful bride so they could live happily ever after together.

It might seem strange for a love song to be in the Bible. What does marriage have to do with God? God says that his people are like a beautiful bride. One day we will be brought together with Jesus like a husband and wife are brought together in marriage. Just like the Shulamite woman loved her groom, we need to love our King Jesus with all of our hearts. Nothing in this world is better than spending time with him.

"I know what I have planned for you," says the Lord. "I have good plans for you. I don't plan to hurt you. I plan to give you hope and a good future. Then you will call my name. You will come to me and pray to me. And I will listen to you. You will search for me. And when you search for me with all your heart, you will find me!"

JEREMIAH 29:11-13

Jeremiah

## Promising Plans

Down In My Heart

*W*hat do Cinderella, Snow White, and Sleeping Beauty have in common? They are all princesses whose stories have happy endings. Even though each of them faced hard times, we love to hear their stories because we know they end well.

*Memory Portion:*
"I know what I have planned for you," says the Lord. "I have good plans for you. I don't plan to hurt you. I plan to give you hope and a good future."

JEREMIAH 29:11

God has planned a wonderful story for your life, too, little princess. He has already written it in his book in heaven. In your life on earth, you will see hard times, just like the fairytale princesses. But the pain will help point you to our Savior and King, Jesus. God promises that your story will have the happiest ending of all. We will get to spend forever in God's kingdom. We will always enjoy his love and the friendship of all the other believers in heaven.

*Heart*

# Amazing Grace

JOHN NEWTON

Amazing Grace!
How sweet the sound—
That saved a wretch like me!
I once was lost, but now am found,
Was blind but now I see.

When we've been there
   ten thousand years,
Bright shining as the sun,
We've no less days to sing God's praise
Than when we'd first begun.

$I$ have hope when I think of this:

The Lord's love never ends.
His mercies never stop.

They are new every morning.
Lord, your loyalty is great.

I say to myself, "The Lord is what
I have left.
So I have hope."

LAMENTATIONS 3:21-24

Lamentations

# Ready, Set, Start Over

$\mathcal{U}$h oh. You goofed again. To make matters worse, it's the same wrong choice you made yesterday. And the day before. And the day before that. At this point, you're not feeling much like God's little princess. You might even be afraid that God (as well as your parents) will just throw you out of the kingdom if you mess up any more. What an awful feeling!

Do you know what is great about God? He's our hero even when we make mistakes again and again. He doesn't keep a list of wrongs. God makes our sins go away for good when we tell him we're sorry and ask him for forgiveness.

Hero

Pretending that we didn't mess up only keeps us from God's forgiveness longer. Tell him the truth today, and ask him for help to make wiser choices next time. Pray that God will make you strong and able to do what is right and good.

The Lord spoke his word to Jonah son of Amittai: "Get up, go to the great city of Nineveh and preach against it. I see the evil things they do."

But Jonah got up to run away from the Lord. He went to the city of Joppa. There he found a ship that was going to the city of Tarshish. Jonah paid for the trip and went aboard. He wanted to go to Tarshish to run away from the Lord.

But the Lord sent a great wind on the sea. This wind made the sea very rough. So the ship was in danger of breaking apart. . . .

Then the men were very afraid. They asked Jonah, "What terrible thing did you do?" They knew Jonah was running away from the Lord because Jonah had told them....

Jonah said to them, "Pick me up, and throw me into the sea. Then it will calm down. I know it is my fault that this great storm has come on you."

... Then the men picked up Jonah and threw him into the sea. So the sea became calm....

And the Lord caused a very big fish to swallow Jonah. Jonah was in the stomach of the fish three days and three nights.

JONAH 1:1-4, 10, 12, 15, 17

# Heavenly Hide and Seek

**Worthy of Love**

You could find them at school. You may see them at church. They may even be in your own home! Some kids are just shy. They are afraid to make new friends. Instead of playing with the others, they will stay by themselves. They may look fine, but don't be fooled. They really want a friend.

Did you know that God wants us to play the hide and seek game? He wants us to look for other people who may be hiding from everyone else. He wants us to look for people who may be lonely or hurting.

*H*e wants us to find them and share his love with them. Invite them to your house. Play with them at school. Let them know they don't need to be afraid. God cares about them and you do, too.

What about you? Are you the one who sometimes feels afraid? Are you so shy you can't make friends? Ask Jesus to help you be brave. Ask him to help you get your thoughts off of yourself. Instead, think about others like you who need a friend. Then pray that God will open your eyes to find those who need to be loved. Begin God's game of hide and seek. You never know who will be "it" next!

When you pray, you should pray like this:

'Our Father in heaven,
we pray that your name will always
    be kept holy.

We pray that your kingdom will come.
We pray that what you want will be done,
here on earth as it is in heaven.

Give us the food we need for each day.

Forgive the sins we have done,
just as we have forgiven those who did
    wrong to us.

Do not cause us to be tested;
but save us from the Evil One.'
[The kingdom, the power, and the glory
are yours forever. Amen.]

MATTHEW 6:9-13

# Praying Like Jesus

**Down In My Heart**

You are a princess, but your kingdom is not of this world. You belong to Jesus, and Jesus' kingdom is in heaven and in people's hearts. God wants us to pray that his kingdom will grow.

*Memory Portion:*
We pray that your kingdom will come. We pray that what you want will be done, here on earth as it is in heaven.

MATTHEW 6:10

139

Jesus uses our prayers to help build his kingdom here on earth. He grows his kingdom by changing people's hearts and helping them to love him. This special prayer that Jesus taught us helps us to remember that God is busy at work adding royal subjects to his kingdom. Prayer allows us to become a part of his great work.

Heart

# Activity

Can you think of anyone in your life who does not know Jesus? Ask your mom to write their names on a note card. Pray for each person every night of the week. Ask Jesus to help those people come to know him. Ask him to change their hearts and add them to his kingdom.

"Everyone who hears these things I say and obeys them is like a wise man. The wise man built his house on rock. It rained hard and the water rose. The winds blew and hit that house. But the house did not fall, because the house was built on rock. But the person who hears the things I teach and does not obey them is like a foolish man. The foolish man built his house on sand. It rained hard, the water rose, and the winds blew and hit that house. And the house fell with a big crash."

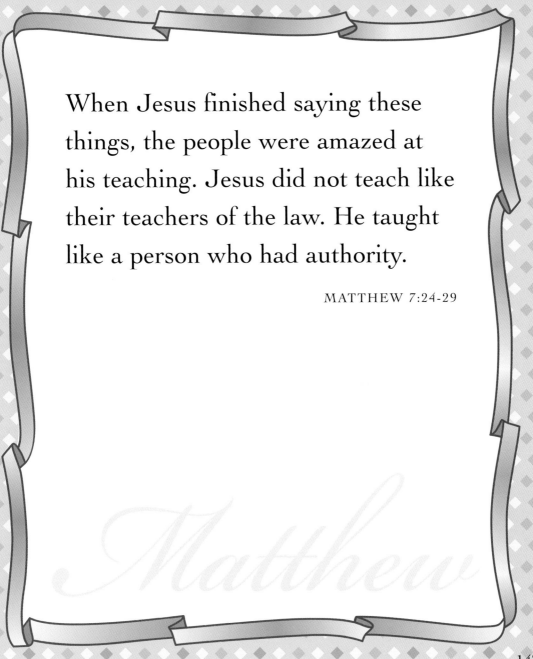

When Jesus finished saying these things, the people were amazed at his teaching. Jesus did not teach like their teachers of the law. He taught like a person who had authority.

MATTHEW 7:24-29

# Teachable Hearts

Princess Charming

You've just finished cleaning your room so you can play outside. You tell your mom, but she thinks you have more work to do. She begins to point out more things that need to be put away. You:

**A** Listen patiently, and clean the rest of the room.

**B** Wait until she leaves, and stuff it all under the bed.

**C** Argue with her, telling her she is wrong and the room is clean.

**D** Start crying because you want to go outside right now.

Do you like to be wrong? Nobody does! We like to think that we know how to do everything. We also like to think that we do everything perfectly. The truth is that no one but God is perfect. The rest of us have a lot of learning to do. God says that he wants us to have teachable hearts. When we mess up, we don't need to cover it up. We just need to admit the problem, and let people like our parents teach us the right and better way. Teachable hearts please God and help us become wiser, smarter, and able to do better work!

Jesus got into a boat, and his followers went with him. A very bad storm arose on the lake. The waves covered the boat. But Jesus was sleeping. The followers went to Jesus and woke him. They said, "Lord, save us! We will drown!"

Jesus answered, "Why are you afraid? You don't have enough faith." Then Jesus got up and gave a command to the wind and the sea. The wind stopped, and the sea became very calm.

The men were amazed. They said, "What kind of man is this? Even the wind and the sea obey him!"

MATTHEW 8:23-27

## Why Worry?

*J*esus' follow-
ers were afraid.
A terrible storm
raged around them.
They were in a small fishing boat.
They thought that they were going
to die. What was Jesus doing
about it? Sleeping! Jesus wasn't
worried. He knew who was in
charge. He knew that the heavenly
Father was taking care of all of
them.

Jesus then showed his power,
too. When he awoke, he spoke to
the wind and waves. They obeyed
him and became still.

$\mathcal{J}$esus reminded his followers (and us) that he is King and controls all things. We don't have to be afraid of sicknesses, storms, accidents, or bad people. Just like the famous song says, God has the whole world in his hands. Only what God allows to happen for his great plan will happen!

*Adore*

# Activity

Sing the song, *He's Got the Whole World in His Hands*. Now think of some things that worry you. Add each item to the verse, and sing it out loud. Remember, God holds everything in his hands!

Jesus used stories to teach them many things. He said: "A farmer went out to plant his seed. While he was planting, some seed fell by the road. The birds came and ate all that seed. Some seed fell on rocky ground, where there wasn't enough dirt. That seed grew very fast, because the ground was not deep. But when the sun rose, the plants dried up because they did not have deep roots. Some other seed fell among thorny weeds. The weeds grew and choked the good plants. Some other seed fell on good ground where it grew and became grain. Some plants made 100 times more grain. Other plants made 60 times more grain, and some made 30 times more grain."

MATTHEW 13:3-8

# A Sweet Surprise

Take a Bow

**What you will need:**

- several packs of fun-sized M&Ms™
- yellow hat or cape
- table
- feather
- rocks
- weeds/plant (fake or real)

*Directions: Mom will be the farmer in the story. Your little princess will act out the different scenes involving the seeds. Have her go in the yard to gather a few rocks and weeds or leaves for your story.*

＊Before the play begins, use tape or string to divide your kitchen table into four areas. Place a feather in the first section. In the next section place a few rocks. In the third section, place dandelions, weeds, leaves, or artificial plants. In the fourth section, put down several M&M™ packets.

**Mom:** *(Start at the first section of the table.)* "I am a farmer, and I need to plant my seeds. I think I'll spread some over here on this road." *(Toss a few M&Ms™ on the first section.)*

**Princess:** *(Act like a bird. Come swooping across the room and eat the M&Ms™.)*

**Mom:** "Oh, the birds have eaten my seed! Well, I'll try some seeds on this rocky soil." *(Put candy beside rocks in second section.)*

151

**Princess:** *(Put on yellow cape or hat, and pretend to be the sun. Shine over the seeds.)*

**Mom:** "Oh, the sun has dried up the plants because the soil was too thin." *(Remove the M&Ms™.)* "I'd better put some seeds here." *(Put candy into third section beside the weeds.)*

**Princess:** *(Take the "seeds" and swallow them.)*

**Mom:** "What happened to the seeds?"

**Princess:** "They have been swallowed up by weeds and are gone now."

**Mom:** "I know. I should try the good soil." *(Sprinkle some candy in the fourth section.)* "What do you see?"

**Princess:** "The seeds have grown, and now there are many! We should plant more here!"

**Take a Bow!!**

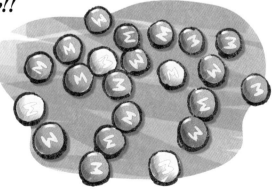

# Role Review

**What does the seed represent?**
*(God's Word)*

**Why did some get eaten by birds?**
*(It never took root. Satan tries to steal away the truth.)*

**Why did some dry up?** *(They didn't have enough dirt. We need to not only hear God's Word, but also to study it and obey it.)*

**Why did some get choked by weeds?**
*(They were too close to danger. We need to watch out for evil in the world.)*

**What made the seeds grow?**
*(Good soil; when we hear and obey God's Word, we bear lots of fruit.)*

Late that afternoon, his followers came to Jesus and said, "No one lives in this place. And it is already late. Send the people away so they can go to the towns and buy food for themselves."

Jesus answered, "They don't need to go away. You give them some food to eat."

The followers answered, "But we have only five loaves of bread and two fish."

Jesus said, "Bring the bread and the fish to me." Then he told the people to sit down on the grass. He took the five loaves of bread and the two fish. Then he looked to heaven and thanked God for the food. Jesus divided the loaves of bread. He gave them to his followers, and they gave the bread to the people.

MATTHEW 14:15-19

154

# Being (and Singing)
## the Blessing

*I* magine this: Your mom has packed you a pretty good lunch. You've traveled far to hear Jesus, and now you are really hungry. Just when you're about to take a bite, you hear someone asking around if anyone has any food to share. Would you want to hide what you have, or give it away to be a blessing?

We need to remember that every good thing in our lives comes from our heavenly Father. He always gives us what we need. We don't have to protect ourselves. We can freely give away God's blessings to help others. God will use our gifts to grow his kingdom and help make our hearts more like his.

## Activity

Is it sometimes hard for you to share? Certain songs help remind us that all our blessings come from God. Sing the song, *Praise God from Whom All Blessings Flow* (called the Doxology), whenever you are tempted to keep the good stuff for yourself. Watch how God can use your little gift to bless others in big ways.

# Doxology

THOMAS KEN

Praise God, from whom
all blessings flow;
Praise Him all creatures here below;
Praise Him above, ye heav'nly hosts;
Praise Father, Son, and Holy Ghost.
Amen.

ACanaanite woman . . . came to Jesus. The woman cried out, "Lord, Son of David, please help me! My daughter has a demon, and she is suffering very much."

. . . Jesus answered, "God sent me only to the lost sheep, the people of Israel."

Then the woman came to Jesus again. She bowed before him and said, "Lord, help me!"

Jesus answered, "It is not right to take the children's bread and give it to the dogs."

The woman said, "Yes, Lord, but even the dogs eat the pieces of food that fall from their masters' table."

Then Jesus answered, "Woman, you have great faith! I will do what you asked me to do." And at that moment the woman's daughter was healed.

MATTHEW 15:22, 24-28

## Ask and Receive

**Princess Charming**

*Y*ou have been playing hard outside with your friends. Suddenly, you realize you are very thirsty. You rush inside the house for relief. You should:

**A** Yell for your mom and tell her, "I'm thirsty."

**B** Tell your mom, "I want something to drink."

**C** Ask your mom, "May I please have something to drink?"

It might not seem easy to see any difference between asking and telling. After all, if you tell your mom you're thirsty, she should know you need something to drink, right? Wrong! As a polite princess, you do not need to demand your way. Remember that your mom has needs, too. She needs your respect. When you ask her for help with polite words like "please" and "thank you," you are showing her respect. Those same magic words work wonders with all grown-ups, and even with other kids!

Jesus was in Bethany. He was at the house of Simon, who had a harmful skin disease. While Jesus was there, a woman came to him. She had an alabaster jar filled with expensive perfume. She poured this perfume on Jesus' head while he was eating.

His followers saw the woman do this and were upset. They asked, "Why waste that perfume? It could be sold for a great deal of money, and the money could be given to the poor."

But Jesus knew what happened. He said, "Why are you troubling this woman? She did a very beautiful thing for me. . . . I tell you the truth. The Good News will be told to people in all the world. And in every place where it is preached, what this woman has done will be told. And people will remember her."

MATTHEW 26:6-10, 13

*But thanks be to God, who always leads us in victory through Christ. God uses us to spread his knowledge everywhere like a sweet-smelling perfume.*

2 CORINTHIANS 2:14

## Something Smells Sweet

**Beauty Secrets**

Your mommy is getting ready for a special evening. How can you tell? She is all dressed up. When she walks by you, she smells wonderful. Soon, the whole house is filled with her wonderful scent.

God has a special perfume for his little princesses, too. But it's not the kind in a bottle. God's Spirit in our hearts is like a special fragrance. When we obey God and share his love with others, our lives smell just as sweet as perfume to God. Other people around us smell it, too. It makes them want to know Jesus.

*Beauty*

Each time you smell your mom's perfume, remember that God has put his Spirit in you if you are his child. Ask God to make your life a sweet-smelling scent to him and a fragrance that will cause others to want to know him.

The day after the Sabbath day was the first day of the week. At dawn on the first day, Mary Magdalene and another woman named Mary went to look at the tomb.

At that time there was a strong earthquake. An angel of the Lord came down from heaven. The angel went to the tomb and rolled the stone away from the entrance. Then he sat on the stone. He was shining as bright as lightning. His clothes were white as snow. The soldiers guarding the tomb were very frightened of the angel. They shook with fear and then became like dead men.

The angel said to the women, "Don't be afraid. I know that you are looking for Jesus, the one who was killed on the cross. But he is not here. He has risen from death as he said he would. Come and see the place where his body was. . . ."

The women left the tomb quickly. They were afraid, but they were also very happy. They ran to tell Jesus' followers what had happened. Suddenly, Jesus met them and said, "Greetings." The women came up to Jesus, took hold of his feet, and worshiped him. Then Jesus said to them, "Don't be afraid. Go and tell my brothers to go on to Galilee. They will see me there."

MATTHEW 28:1-6, 8-10

# Easter Son-Rise

Take a Bow

*Directions: Roll the blanket or sleeping bag to create a makeshift tomb. Gently lay the pillow over the opening. Mom plays the angel first, then Jesus. Princess plays the role of women visiting the tomb.*

**What you will need:**
- large, thick blanket or sleeping bag
- pillow
- dress-up wings or white dress
- scarf or shawl
- sash
- jar with cloves, cinnamon, or other spices

**Princess** *(clothed with a shawl or hood)*: "The Sabbath is over. Sunday is here. Now we can go to Jesus' tomb to put spices on his body." *(Take the jar of spices and walk to the tomb.)*

**Mom** *(dressed in white or with wings)*: *(Take the "stone" away from the tomb and sit on it.)* "Don't be afraid. I know that you are looking for Jesus, the One who was killed on the cross. But he is not here. He has risen from death as he said he would. Come and see the place where his body was."

**Princess:** *(Run to the tomb and look inside.)* "He isn't here!"

**Mom:** "Go quickly and tell his followers. Say to them, 'Jesus has risen from death. He is going into Galilee.

168

He will be there before you. You will see him there.'"

**Princess:** "We will go at once." *(Turn around and begin walking in the other direction.)*

**Mom** *(now wearing sash, as Jesus)*: "Greetings!"

**Princess:** "Jesus! You're alive!" *(Bow down and hold his feet.)*

**Mom** *(as Jesus)*: "Don't be afraid. Go and tell my brothers to go on to Galilee. They will see me there."

**Take a Bow!!**

## Role Review

Who went to visit Jesus' tomb? *(Mary Magdalene and the other Mary)*

What did they find when they got there? *(an empty tomb with an angel beside it)*

What news did the angel have for them? *(Jesus was no longer dead. He would meet his followers in Galilee.)*

Who else did the women see? *(Jesus)*

How was his message similar to the angel's? *(Both said not to be afraid and that Jesus would meet his followers in Galilee.)*

Why was it important for Jesus to live again? *(It shows he really is God, what he says is true, and he has defeated death for him and us.)*

A ruler from the synagogue, named Jairus, came to that place. Jairus saw Jesus and bowed before him. The ruler begged Jesus again and again. He said, "My little daughter is dying. Please come and put your hands on her. Then she will be healed and will live." So Jesus went with the ruler, and many people followed Jesus. They were pushing very close around him....

Some men came from the house of Jairus, the synagogue ruler. The men said. "Your daughter is dead. There is now no need to bother the teacher."

But Jesus paid no attention to what the men said. He said to the synagogue ruler, "Don't be afraid; only believe."

...They came to the house of the synagogue ruler, and Jesus found many people there crying loudly....

Then he took hold of the girl's hand and said to her, "Talitha, koum!" (This means, "Little girl, I tell you to stand up!") The girl stood right up and began walking. (She was 12 years old.) The father and mother and the followers were amazed.

MARK 5:22-24, 35-36, 38, 41-42

# No Small Miracle

Take a Bow

*Directions: The princess plays the part of both Jairus and his daughter. Mom wears the hood and acts as Jesus. Feel free to swap roles and repeat the play a second time!*

**What you will need:**
- crown
- scarf or sash
- bed

**Princess** *(wearing crown)*: "Jesus, Jesus! I am Jairus, a ruler in the Temple." *(Bow down to the ground in front of mom.)* "Please! I need your help! My little girl is dying! Please come and put your hands on her. Then she will be healed and live!"

**Mom** *(wearing scarf as a sash)*: "Yes, Jairus. I will come with you."

**Princess:** "My house is this way." *(Lead mom around the room until you come near the bed.)*

"Oh, no! I hear crying! Everyone is saying my little girl has already died! We're too late!"

**Mom:** "Why are they crying and making so much noise? This child is not dead. She is only asleep. Have everyone leave the room."

*(Princess changes from Jairus to his little girl. Lie down on the bed and pretend to be dead.)*

172

**Mom** *(taking the girl's hand)*: "Little girl, I tell you to stand up!"

**Princess** *(getting up, stretching, and walking around the room)*: "I am well! And I'm very hungry."

**Mom:** "Your parents will give you food. Be careful not to tell anyone what has happened here today."

***Take a Bow!!***

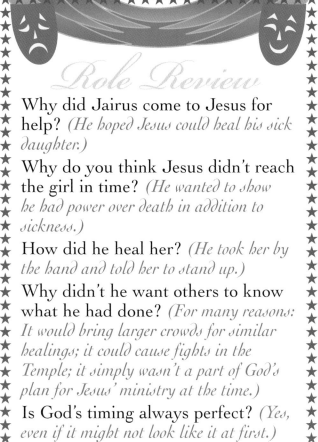

## Role Review

Why did Jairus come to Jesus for help? *(He hoped Jesus could heal his sick daughter.)*

Why do you think Jesus didn't reach the girl in time? *(He wanted to show he had power over death in addition to sickness.)*

How did he heal her? *(He took her by the hand and told her to stand up.)*

Why didn't he want others to know what he had done? *(For many reasons: It would bring larger crowds for similar healings; it could cause fights in the Temple; it simply wasn't a part of God's plan for Jesus' ministry at the time.)*

Is God's timing always perfect? *(Yes, even if it might not look like it at first.)*

Jesus and his followers went to Capernaum and went into a house there. Then Jesus said to them, "What were you arguing about on the road?" But the followers did not answer, because their argument on the road was about which one of them was the greatest.

Jesus sat down and called the 12 apostles to him. He said, "If anyone wants to be the most important, then he must be last of all and servant of all."

MARK 9:33-35

## It's Your Serve

**Worthy of Love**

It's one thing if you're an only child. But being kind and putting others first becomes a lot harder when you have brothers and sisters. After all, aren't you important, too? Why should they get to enjoy being the first in line while you wait?

You are important. So is Jesus. In fact, as Creator of the world and as the Son of God, he is *most* important.

Even though he is King of the whole universe, he still came to earth as a servant. He even gave up his life for us while we were still sinful and disobedient people.

Jesus says that his people need to serve others the same way. So today, let your sister go first at the computer. Let your brother have a first turn on the bike. In fact, make a game out of finding all the different ways you can serve the different members of your family.

Love

At the end of the day, count them up. Then thank God for giving you the chance to serve others and put them first, just like Jesus does for us.

Some people brought their small children to Jesus so he could touch them. But his followers told the people to stop bringing their children to him. When Jesus saw this, he was displeased. He said to them, "Let the little children come to me. Don't stop them. The kingdom of God belongs to people who are like these little children. I tell you the truth. You must accept the kingdom of God as a little child accepts things, or you will never enter it." Then Jesus took the children in his arms. He put his hands on them and blessed them.

MARK 10:13-16

*I Adore You!*

*Y*ou've sung the song a million times: *Jesus Loves Me.* But how can you know it's true? If you came face to face with Jesus, would he give you a great big hug or push you aside to do more important work?

As the song says, God's Word tells us the truth. Several small children actually had the chance to see Jesus' love for them. They came up to Jesus. Some crawled into his lap. Others sat at his feet.

Jesus' followers told them to go away. They thought Jesus was too busy. Jesus said, "Let the little children come to me." He is never too busy for children. He loves them deeply, and he wants them to come to him.

*Adore*

# Activity

Why don't you come to him right now in prayer and praise? Sing *Jesus Loves Me* to him. Thank him for his love. Then add verses of your own that will help you remember how special you are to God.

Jesus said to the followers, "Go everywhere in the world. Tell the Good News to everyone. Anyone who believes and is baptized will be saved. But he who does not believe will be judged guilty."

. . . After the Lord Jesus said these things to the followers he was carried up into heaven. There, Jesus sat at the right side of God. The followers went everywhere in the world and told the Good News to people. And the Lord helped them. The Lord proved that the Good News they told was true by giving them power to work miracles.

MARK 16:15-16, 19-20

> *How beautiful is the one who announces peace. He brings good news and announces salvation. How beautiful are the feet of the one who says to Jerusalem, "Your God is king."*
>
> ISAIAH 52:7

## Fancy Feet

**Beauty Secrets**

Can you imagine Cinderella going to the royal ball without her glass slippers? No matter where we are headed, we need our shoes! They protect our feet and provide a fun way to show our style.

183

id you know that God has special shoes for princess feet? He says that the best shoes are spiritual ones. They tell others the Good News about Jesus. They also protect us from believing lies about God. Wherever we walk, we need to be ready to explain to others why Jesus is our King and why his way is best. God says that feet that run to other people to share his love are the most beautiful feet in the world!

*Beauty*

_Beauty Tips_

Soak your feet in a warm bubble bath tonight. Follow up with some good foot lotion. As you soak and rub your feet, talk to God. Ask him to direct your feet to the people who need to hear about him. Then ask for wisdom to know how to share his love with them.

Zechariah and Elizabeth truly did what God said was good. They did everything the Lord commanded and told people to do. They were without fault in keeping his law. But Zechariah and Elizabeth had no children. Elizabeth could not have a baby; and both of them were very old....

On the right side of the incense table, an angel of the Lord came and stood before Zechariah. When he saw the angel, Zechariah was confused and frightened. But the angel said to him, "Zechariah, don't be afraid.

Your prayer has been heard by God. Your wife, Elizabeth, will give birth to a son. You will name him John...."

Later, Zechariah's wife, Elizabeth, became pregnant. She did not go out of her house for five months. Elizabeth said, "Look what the Lord has done for me! My people were ashamed of me, but now the Lord has taken away that shame."

LUKE 1:6-7, 11-13, 24-25

*(For more of this story, read all of Luke 1.)*

*Luke*

# Elizabeth, God's Prime-Time Princess

**Bible Princesses**

It was way past time for Elizabeth to have a baby.

She was old now. She needed to put that dream behind her and move on.

God had different plans, though. He used an angel to tell her husband, Zechariah, the good news. God was going to give them a special baby in their old age! Zechariah didn't believe it, so he lost his ability to speak. Elizabeth rejoiced in the news! They both obeyed God and named the baby John. Zechariah got his voice back.

*Princesses*

John became known as John the Baptist. He was the famous prophet who got the people ready to hear about Jesus.

Do you have a hard time waiting for good things? God has his own schedule, and we need to follow it. When you find yourself in a hurry to get your own way, ask God to forgive you. Ask him for patience to wait on him. God's timing is always perfect and brings the greatest blessing.

189

The angel said to her, "Don't be afraid, Mary, because God is pleased with you. Listen! You will become pregnant. You will give birth to a son, and you will name him Jesus. He will be great, and people will call him the Son of the Most High. The Lord God will give him the throne of King David, his ancestor. He will rule over the people of Jacob forever. His kingdom will never end."

. . . Mary said, "I am the servant girl of the Lord. Let this happen to me as you say!" Then the angel went away.

LUKE 1:30-33, 38

*Luke*

*It is not fancy hair, gold jewelry, or fine clothes that should make you beautiful. No, your beauty should come from within you—the beauty of a gentle and quiet spirit. This beauty will never disappear, and it is worth very much to God.*

1 PETER 3:3-4

## Heart Makeovers

**Beauty Secrets**

Don't you just love dressing up? Almost all little girls love to put on make-up, jewelry, and fancy clothes, and style their hair in a most princess-like fashion. Truth is, even grown-up girls love to look their best.

id you know that God wants us to be beautiful, too? He's the One who put the desire in our hearts. But real beauty isn't something we put on the outside of our bodies. We are most beautiful when our hearts are obedient to God. His love shines through us in our words and actions. Beautiful hearts never fade with age.

## Beauty

# Beauty Tips

Think of some ways your mom shows you her beautiful heart. Tell her what you see. Ask God to work in your heart to make you beautiful on the inside, too.

When Elizabeth heard Mary's greeting, the unborn baby inside Elizabeth jumped. Then Elizabeth was filled with the Holy Spirit. She cried out in a loud voice, "God has blessed you more than any other woman. And God has blessed the baby which you will give birth to. You are the mother of my Lord, and you have come to me! Why has something so good happened to me? When I heard your voice, the baby inside me jumped with joy. You are blessed because you believed what the Lord said to you would really happen."

Then Mary said,
"My soul praises the Lord;

my heart is happy because
God is my Savior.

I am not important, but God has
shown his care for me, his servant
girl.

From now on, all people will say
that I am blessed,

because the Powerful One has done
great things for me.

His name is holy."

LUKE 1:41-49

*Luke*

# Mary, Mother of King Jesus

**Bible Princesses**

She was just an ordinary girl who lived in Nazareth, a town in Galilee. She had simple plans to get married and have a family. But God's angel changed the picture. He told her that God had noticed her. He had chosen her for royalty. She would be the mother of God's King and Savior, Jesus. She would give birth to a miracle. She would have the joy of teaching the Creator how to live in the world he himself had made.

Princesses

It's hard to understand how God could come to earth as a human baby. Mary didn't understand, either. What she did know was that God was in charge. She trusted him to do what was right. She simply obeyed with a servant heart.

We won't always understand God's plan, either. Like Mary, we do need to trust that God knows what he is doing. Follow God's leading in your life by reading his Word, the Bible.

Jesus said, "There were two men. Both men owed money to the same banker. One man owed the banker 500 silver coins. The other man owed the banker 50 silver coins. The men had no money; so they could not pay what they owed. But the banker told the men that they did not have to pay him. Which one of the two men will love the banker more?"

Simon, the Pharisee, answered, "I think it would be the one who owed him the most money."

Jesus said to Simon "You are right."

LUKE 7:41-43

## Forgive and Forget

**Worthy of Love**

You are playing nicely at home. You didn't even do anything mean. Suddenly, your sister grabs your toy and begins playing with it. What's worse is that this is the third time she's done it today. What should you do?

You could scream. You could tattle. Or you can do what Jesus says. He wants us to forgive. He wants us to love others so much that we no longer remember the bad things they have done to us. It's okay to talk it out.

$\mathcal{I}$t's good to let others know how you feel. But no matter how they act, we need to be like Jesus. When you forgive someone for being mean to you—even if they aren't sorry—you are showing God's love. It also shows you have a thankful heart for the way God always forgives you when you sin.

The next time your friends or siblings make you mad, stop for a moment. Before you go tell on them or yell at them, remember Jesus.

*Love*

Think about how he died on the cross just so God could forgive your sin. What an amazing act of love that was! Ask Jesus for strength to forgive others the way he forgives you.

The Pharisees and the teachers of the law began to complain: "Look! This man welcomes sinners and even eats with them!"

Then Jesus told them this story: "Suppose one of you has 100 sheep, but he loses 1 of them. Then he will leave the other 99 sheep alone and go out and look for the lost sheep. The man will keep on searching for the lost sheep until he finds it. And when he finds it, the man is very happy. He puts it on his shoulders and goes home. He calls to his friends and neighbors and says, 'Be happy with me because I found my lost sheep!'

In the same way, I tell you there is much joy in heaven when 1 sinner changes his heart. There is more joy for that 1 sinner than there is for 99 good people who don't need to change.

"Suppose a woman has ten silver coins, but she loses one of them. She will light a lamp and clean the house. She will look carefully for the coin until she finds it. And when she finds it, she will call her friends and neighbors and say, 'Be happy with me because I have found the coin that I lost!' In the same way, there is joy before the angels of God when 1 sinner changes his heart."

LUKE 15:2-10

# Lost and Found

Take a Bow

*Directions: Mom plays the part of Jesus. The princess is the shepherd and the woman. This short play is also a game. Before it begins, mom hides the sheep somewhere in the room when the princess isn't looking. Play it as many times as the princess desires!*

**What you will need:**
- plastic or stuffed animal sheep
- walking stick or staff
- 10 silver quarters or nickels
- scarf or hood

**Mom** *(as Jesus, wearing a hood)*:
"I know you wonder why I welcome sinners to come to me. I even eat with them. Suppose one of you has a hundred sheep and loses one of them. What would you do?"

**Princess** *(holding the staff)*:
"96, 97, 98, 99…where is 100? Where is my precious little lamb? I cannot lose a single sheep. I must go and find it."

*(Princess searches room until she finds the hidden sheep.)*

"I've found it! The sheep that was lost has been found." *(Run to mom.)* "Come with me and have a party! I have found my lost sheep!"

**Mom:** "I tell you there is much joy in heaven when one sinner changes his heart. There is more joy for that one sinner than

204

there is for 99 good people who don't need to change."

*(Hide one coin while princess is out of the room, then begin again.)*
"Suppose a woman has ten silver coins, but loses one of them. What will she do?"

**Princess:** *(Count out the nine coins on the table.)* "No matter how many times I count, I only see nine coins. Where is the tenth? I must go find it!" *(Leave the 9 coins on the table and search for the lost/hidden coin.)*

"At last I've found my missing coin! Come, neighbors and friends, and have a party with me! I have found my lost coin!"

**Mom:** "In the same way, there is joy before the angels of God when one sinner changes his heart."

### *Take a Bow!!*

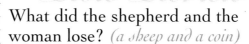

*Role Review*

What did the shepherd and the woman lose? *(a sheep and a coin)*

Why did they go looking for what was lost? *(It was special to them.)*

Was Jesus really concerned about animals and money, or was he picturing something else? *(The sheep and coin were pictures of people who had sinned and turned away from God.)*

Why was Jesus telling this story to the Pharisees? *(He wanted them to know that God loves us even when we sin. It also shows that God chases us to bring us back to him when we are lost in our sins. We don't seek him on our own.)*

Jesus said, "A man had two sons. The younger son said to his father, 'Give me my share of the property.' So the father divided the property between his two sons. Then the younger son gathered up all that was his and left. He traveled far away to another country. There he wasted his money in foolish living.... The son realized that he had been very foolish. He thought, 'All of my father's servants have plenty of food. But I am here, almost dying with hunger. I will leave and return to my father. I'll say to him: Father, I have sinned against God and against you....' So the son left and went to his father.

"While the son was still a long way off, his father saw him coming.... So the father ran to him, and hugged and kissed him.... The father said to his servants,... My son was dead, but now he is alive again! He was lost, but now he is found! So they began to celebrate.'"

LUKE 15:11-13, 17-18, 20, 22, 24

206

# Forgiving Family

Take a Bow

*Directions: Mom will play the father. Princess will be the younger son who runs away. Have the pigs (or other stuffed animals) staged in a corner of the room. Keep the robe, ring, and sandals for later in the play.*

**What you will need:**
- play money (from a board game)
- stuffed animal pigs (or any other kind)
- robe
- ring
- sandals

**Princess:** *(Cross your arms and act angry.)* "I want to get out of here! Give me my share of the property so I can leave."

**Mom** *(looking sad)*: "If that is what you truly want, then here." *(Hand her play money.)*

**Princess:** "At last! I'm on my own." *(Wander around the room. Pretend to spend money in different places.)* "This might make me happy. I'll spend some money here." *(Walk around some more.)* "This should make me happy. I'll buy this." *(Spend more money until it's all gone.)*

"Oh, no! I've run out of money! I'd better get a job."

*(Walk over to the pigs. Begin feeding them.)*

"I've been so foolish! My father's servants have plenty of

207

food, but I am here, dying of hunger! I must go back home and tell my Father I've sinned. Maybe he will let me be one of his servants, and at least I won't be hungry." *(Turn around and walk back to the father.)*

**Mom:** *(Cup hand over eyes as if looking in the distance.)* "Son, is that you?" *(Run over to princess, and give her a big hug and kiss.)*

**Princess:** "I have sinned against God and you. I am not worthy to be called your son."

**Mom:** *(Put robe, ring, and sandals on princess while you speak.)* "Hurry, servants! Bring the best clothes and put them on him. Put a ring on his finger and sandals on his feet. Get our fat calf and kill it. It's time for a feast! My son was dead, but now he is alive again! He was lost, but now he is found!"

***Take a Bow!!***

# Role Review

**Why did the son leave?** *(He thought he would be happier being somewhere else.)*

**What are some ways that we leave God?** *(whenever we disobey and do what we want)*

**Was the son happier away from his father?** *(No; he couldn't live without him.)*

**How did the father act when the son came home?** *(He had been waiting for him. He ran to meet him with hugs and kisses. Then he dressed him and had a party to welcome him home.)*

**If you sin, what should you do?** *(Turn back to God, my heavenly Father.)*

**How will God act toward you?** *(He will be just like the father in the story.)*

Jesus was on his way to Jerusalem. Traveling from Galilee to Samaria, he came into a small town. Ten men met him there. These men did not come close to Jesus, because they all had a harmful skin disease. But they called to him, "Jesus! Master! Please help us!"

When Jesus saw the men, he said, "Go and show yourselves to the priests."

While the ten men were going, they were healed. When one of them saw that he was healed, he went back to Jesus. He praised God in a loud voice. Then he bowed down at Jesus' feet and thanked him. (This man was a Samaritan.) Jesus asked, "Ten men were healed; where are the other nine? Is this Samaritan the only one who came back to thank God?" Then Jesus said to him, "Stand up and go on your way. You were healed because you believed."

LUKE 17:11-19

*Luke*

# Return the Favor

**Princess Charming**

You've come inside from playing, and you're starving. You notice that mom has made you a snack, which you happily eat. Now that you are finished, you:

**A** Get up and run back outside.

**B** Get out some games to play on the table.

**C** Clean up your mess and tell mom, "Thank you!"

It might seem like magic. When mom is around, food just appears. The house gets cleaned. And life is a lot of fun. But as a reigning princess, you need to remember: Your mom and dad work hard to make your castle a place you love. You can show them a grateful heart by helping them, too. Pick up after yourself. Clear your plate. Make up your bed. It might seem little and unimportant at the time. But small acts of service help others in a big way. Saying "thanks" shows that you notice others and care about them, too.

Jesus saw some rich people putting their gifts into the Temple money box. Then Jesus saw a poor widow. She put two small copper coins into the box. He said, "I tell you the truth. This poor widow gave only two small coins. But she really gave more than all those rich people. The rich have plenty; they gave only what they did not need. This woman is very poor, but she gave all she had. And she needed that money to live on."

LUKE 21:1-4

# The Gift of Giving

When someone hands you a pack of your favorite candy, what is the last thing you really want to do? Does your mom or dad have to make you share, or do you do it with a happy heart?

Jesus knew that we don't like to give away the stuff we really like.

It's hard to share because we're afraid we'll lose what we think we need. But God wants us to trust him to meet our needs. If we really believe God will provide what is best for us, then we are freed to share what we have with others in need. When we share what we have, it pleases God, blesses others, and makes us feel good inside.

Truths

## Make It Yours

What made Jesus so happy about the widow's offering? Was he more concerned with how much she gave or how willing she was to give? You might not think that you have anything to give, either. But you do! You can share your toys, clothes, candy, or anything else you have with others in need. You can give a kind word or loving hug. You can give your time to help someone else. Like the widow, give whatever you do have with a grateful heart!

They found that the stone had been rolled away from the entrance of the tomb. They went in, but they did not find the body of the Lord Jesus. While they were wondering about this, two men in shining clothes suddenly stood beside them. The women were very afraid; they bowed their heads to the ground. The men said to the women, "Why are you looking for a living person here? This is a place for the dead. Jesus is not here. He has risen from death! Do you remember what he said in Galilee?"

...These women were Mary Magdalene, Joanna, Mary the mother of James, and some other women. The women told the apostles everything that had happened at the tomb.

LUKE 24:2-6, 10

*When you talk, do not say harmful things. But say what people need—words that will help others become stronger. Then what you say will help those who listen to you.*

EPHESIANS 4:29

## Beautiful Lips

**Beauty Secrets**

No makeover is quite complete without a colorful touch of lipstick. Red, pink, orange . . . the options are endless. It's cool to match the colors with our clothes. Really, it's just plain fun to put lipstick on our lips.

Have you ever wondered why we like to color our mouths? The Bible says our mouths are a very important part of our bodies. From them, we can speak words that encourage and bless other people. Or we can sin and use words that hurt others' feelings. Jesus wants us to be very careful to always speak truthful words that help others feel loved. Let your lipstick remind you of what matters most to God. Truly beautiful lips speak loving words that come from a kind heart.

# Beauty Tips

Ask your mom if you can borrow her favorite lipstick to try on just for fun. After you put some on, take a note card and kiss it, leaving the mark of your kiss. Put it by your bathroom mirror to remember what God says. Use your words to build others up with God's good news of love!

Two of Jesus' followers were going to a town named Emmaus. It is about seven miles from Jerusalem. They were talking about everything that had happened. While they were discussing these things, Jesus himself came near and began walking with them. . . .

Then Jesus said to them, "You are foolish and slow to realize what is true. You should believe everything the prophets said. . . . Then Jesus began to explain everything that had been written about himself in the

Scriptures. He started with Moses, and then he talked about what all the prophets had said about him. . . .

And then, they were allowed to recognize Jesus. But when they saw who he was, he disappeared. They said to each other, "When Jesus talked to us on the road, it felt like a fire burning in us. It was exciting when he explained the true meaning of the Scriptures."

LUKE 24:13-15, 25, 27, 31-32

# Charmed, I'm Sure

Princess Charming

Your friend has been working hard on a drawing. You get up to peek over her shoulder and see how she's doing. You decide to say:

A  "That's really great! I like your colors."

B  "What on earth is that? It looks funny."

C  "That's not how you're supposed to do it."

D  "You don't draw very well."

All during the day, you have the chance to talk to other people. You also have a choice. You can say good, kind words that help people. Or you can say things that will hurt their feelings. God says we need to guard our mouths. He wants us to only say words that build others up. He never wants us to tear them down. Ask Jesus to help you see something good in the other person. Then tell that person the good that you see! It helps them, and you become more like Jesus.

Jesus said, "Don't let your hearts be troubled. Trust in God. And trust in me. There are many rooms in my Father's house. I would not tell you this if it were not true. I am going there to prepare a place for you. After I go and prepare a place for you, I will come back. Then I will take you to be with me so that you may be where I am. You know the way to the place where I am going."

Thomas said to Jesus, "Lord, we don't know where you are going. So how can we know the way?"

Jesus answered, "I am the way. And I am the truth and the life. The only way to the Father is through me."

JOHN 14:1-6

# God's Building Blueprint

**My Hero**

Did you know that Jesus had another job besides teaching? He was a carpenter—someone who knew how to build houses, furniture, and other things. He may have built tables, chairs, shelves, and cabinets. The Bible doesn't tell us what he built while he lived on earth. It does tell us that Jesus is busy in heaven building right now. It's very exciting!

227

*J*esus told his disciples that he is in heaven building mansions for all the people who will go to heaven to live with him one day. He wants us all to live together as his special family. When we leave this earth, we will be welcomed home to live with Jesus in the beautiful house he has built for us—the most beautiful home you could imagine. It is made more beautiful because Jesus will be there waiting for us.

*Hero*

What kind of house or apartment do you live in now? How long did it take to be built? God has been building his kingdom for a very long time. When he's finished, it's going to be incredible!

Jesus answered, "I am the way. And I am the truth and the life. The only way to the Father is through me. If you really knew me, then you would know my Father, too. But now you do know him, and you have seen him."

JOHN 14:6-7

*John*

# Only One Shepherd

**Down In My Heart**

Can a kingdom have more than one king? No. In fact, many wars have been fought in lots of places around the world over who should be the one in charge.

*Memory Portion:*

Jesus answered, "I am the way.
And I am the truth and the life.
The only way to the Father
is through me."

JOHN 14:6

Can there be more than one God?
Jesus says no. Some people would like to
believe whatever they want. The truth is
that only the God of the Bible is in charge.
He rules our world from heaven. He says
that we can't get to heaven by being
good. We can't sneak in when he's
not watching. The only
way we can have eter-
nal life with God is by
trusting in Jesus, God's
perfect Son.

*Heart*

## *Blessed Assurance*

FANNY J. CROSBY / PHEOBE P. KNAPP

Blessed assurance, Jesus is mine!
O what a foretaste of glory divine!
Heir of salvation, purchase of God,
Born of His Spirit, washed in His blood!

This is my story, this is my song,
Praising my Savior all the day long;
This is my story, this is my song,
Praising my Savior all the day long.

"If you love me, you will do the things I command. I will ask the Father, and he will give you another Helper. He will give you this Helper to be with you forever. The Helper is the Spirit of truth. The world cannot accept him because it does not see him or know him. But you know him. He lives with you, and he will be in you.

"I will not leave you all alone like orphans. I will come back to you. In a little while the world will not see me anymore, but you will see me. Because I live, you will live, too."

JOHN 14:15-19

# The Great Comeback

When Jesus died on the cross, how do you think his followers felt? Scared? Sad? Lonely? They thought they had lost all hope. They had lost their leader and teacher, but most of all they had lost their best friend. They thought they had been left all alone. Then, Jesus returned from the dead! Now they knew they had hope.

o you ever feel frightened, sad, or alone? Jesus knows how you feel. You are a precious member of his kingdom! Just like he told his followers back then, he reminds us, too. He hasn't left us alone. He is with us every moment of the day. No matter how we're feeling, good or bad, he is right beside us.

Hero

He puts his Holy Spirit in our hearts to help us follow him. And he promises to come back to earth to get us. He'll take us home to heaven to live with him and his people forever.

"I am the vine, and you are the branches. If a person remains in me and I remain in him, then he produces much fruit. But without me he can do nothing. If anyone does not remain in me, then he is like a branch that is thrown away. That branch dies. People pick up dead branches, throw them into the fire and burn them. Remain in me and follow my teachings. If you do this, then you can ask for anything you want, and it will be given to you. You should produce much fruit and show that you are my followers. This brings glory to my Father. I loved you as the Father loved me. Now remain in my love."

JOHN 15:5-9

# The Great Connection

Take a Bow

*Directions: Mom stands tall and straight in the middle of the room. She is the vine for our story. The princess wears a green scarf or clothes to pretend like she is a branch with leaves.*

**Mom:** "I am the vine, and you are the branches." *(Point to your daughter.)* If you stay connected to me, you will grow fruit." *(Hold your daughter's hand. Have her sprout out from the ground, holding fruit.)* "But if you are not connected to me . . ." *(Let go of daughter's hand. Have her drop the fruit and shrivel to the ground.)* "You can do nothing." *(Pick up dead branch.)* "If anyone does not remain in me, then he is like a branch that is thrown away." *(Throw branch to the side.)* "People pick up dead branches and throw them into the fire and burn them."

*(Repeat again, this time with roles reversed. The princess is the vine, and mom is the branches).*

**Princess:** "I am the vine, and you are the branches."

239

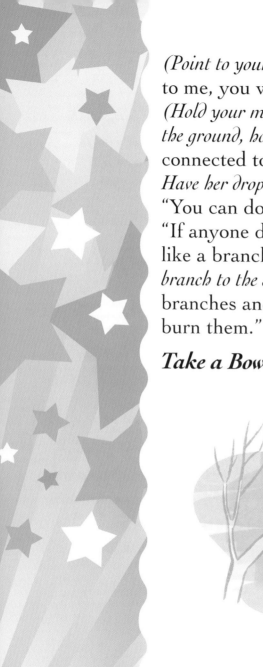

*(Point to your mom.)* "If you stay connected to me, you will grow fruit."
*(Hold your mom's hand. Have her sprout out from the ground, holding fruit.)* "But if you are not connected to me..." *(Let go of mom's hand. Have her drop the fruit and shrivel to the ground.)* "You can do nothing." *(Pick up dead branch.)* "If anyone does not remain in me, then he is like a branch that is thrown away." *(Throw branch to the side.)* "People pick up dead branches and throw them into the fire and burn them."

### Take a Bow!!

# Role Review

What kind of fruit is Jesus talking about? *(good attitudes and actions)*

Can you be a good girl without Jesus' help? *(no)*

Can you love others all by yourself? *(no)*

What disconnects us from Jesus? *(sin, being too busy to remember God and his Word)*

How can you stay connected to Jesus? *(by praying for help, reading his Word, repenting, and obeying)*

What happens to those who don't have Jesus? *(They don't bear fruit or do good things. They are destroyed.)*

A man named Ananias and his wife Sapphira sold some land. But he gave only part of the money to the apostles. He secretly kept some of it for himself. His wife knew about this, and she agreed to it. Peter said, "Ananias, why did you let Satan rule your heart? You lied to the Holy Spirit. Why did you keep part of the money you received for the land for yourself? Before you sold the land, it belonged to you. And even after you sold it, you could have used the money any way you wanted. Why did you think of doing this? You lied to God, not to men!" When Ananias heard this, he fell down and died. Some young men came in, wrapped up his body, carried it out, and buried it. And everyone who heard about this was filled with fear.

ACTS 5:1-6

## Truth Be Told

**Royal Truths**

Isn't your imagination wonderful? We love to dress up and pretend and imagine all kinds of fantastic stories. But keep this truth in mind: We need to remember when it's time to stop dreaming and start being real.

$\mathcal{G}$od says he wants his princesses to always tell the truth. When your parents or teachers ask you to tell them the truth, the time for fantasy is over. Don't make up the answer or pretend you don't know. Do what is right. Tell the truth, and trust your heavenly King to make matters right in the end.

*Truths*

## Make It Yours

The story of Ananias and Sapphira can sound scary. Did they get in trouble because they didn't give all their money away? No. They were punished because they lied to God. They thought they could trick him. We need to remember that God already knows everything. It doesn't make any sense to lie because he knows the truth. Ask God to give you the courage you need to always tell the truth, even when you are afraid.

In the city of Joppa there was a follower named Tabitha. (Her Greek name, Dorcas, means "a deer.") She was always doing good and helping the poor. While Peter was in Lydda, Tabitha became sick and died. Her body was washed and put in a room upstairs. The followers in Joppa heard that Peter was in Lydda. (Lydda is near Joppa.) So they sent two men to Peter. They begged him, "Hurry, please come to us!" Peter got ready and went with them. When he arrived, they took him to the upstairs room. All the widows stood around Peter, crying. They showed him the shirts and coats that Tabitha had made when she was still alive. Peter sent everyone out of the room. He kneeled and prayed. Then he turned to the body and said, "Tabitha, stand up!" She opened her eyes, and when she saw Peter, she sat up.

ACTS 9:36-40

# Care to Be Caring

**Royal Truths**

Why do you like to get gifts? Sure, it's fun to have stuff. It's even more fun to play with it. But we also love to get surprises from other people because we feel loved. We feel like someone cares enough about us to give us a treat.

Did you know that God cares about you? He cares about your thoughts, what makes you happy and sad, and everything else about you. He also wants you to care about other people in the same way. Caring about other people is a sign that God's love lives in your heart. It makes us look at other people's needs instead of our own. It helps us serve other people instead of always trying to get more for ourselves.

Truths

# Make It Yours

Tabitha (also known as Dorcas) loved to care about others. She spent her whole life helping the poor and doing good to everyone around her. How about you? Do you spend more time thinking about what you want or what you can do for others? Ask Jesus to open your eyes. Have him show you how you can better care for your family members and the people around you.

Paul had a vision. In the vision, a man from Macedonia came to him. The man stood there and begged, "Come over to Macedonia. Help us!" After Paul had seen the vision, we immediately prepared to leave for Macedonia. We understood that God had called us to tell the Good News to those people.

We left Troas in a ship, and we sailed straight to the island of Samothrace. The next day we sailed to Neapolis. Then we went by land to Philippi, the leading city in that part of Macedonia. It is also a Roman colony. We stayed there for several days.

On the Sabbath day we went outside the city gate to the river. There we thought we would find a special place for prayer. Some women had gathered there, so we sat down and talked with them. There was a woman named Lydia from the city of Thyatira. Her job was selling purple cloth. She worshiped the true God. The Lord opened her mind to pay attention to what Paul was saying. She and all the people in her house were baptized. Then Lydia invited us to her home. She said, "If you think I am truly a believer in the Lord, then come stay in my house." And she persuaded us to stay with her.

ACTS 16:9-15

# Lydia, the Leader of Light

*L*ydia had an important job in the city of Thyatira. She sold purple cloth to people who could afford it. Her business made her a leader among women. She also loved God very much.

Paul came to her town and told her about Jesus, God's Son. God opened Lydia's heart so that she could understand what Paul was saying. She trusted Jesus to save her from her sins, too. She was eager to help God's people spread the Good News about Jesus.

*Princesses*

Even though it wasn't safe, she invited them to her home. God's people were often killed or put into jail. Lydia didn't care. She loved God more than her life. She always kept her house open to help other believers.

God gives each of us gifts to use for his kingdom. Lydia was a natural leader. She used her gifts to lead others to Jesus. What are your gifts? Will you share them with others to help bring God glory?

Paul and Silas were thrown into jail. The jailer was ordered to guard them carefully. . . .

About midnight Paul and Silas were praying and singing songs to God. . . . Suddenly, there was a big earthquake. It was so strong that it shook the foundation of the jail. Then all the doors of the jail broke open. All the prisoners were freed from their chains. . . .

The jailer told someone to bring a light. Then he ran inside. Shaking with fear, he fell down before Paul and Silas. Then he brought them outside and said, "Men, what must I do to be saved?"

They said to him, "Believe in the Lord Jesus and you will be saved—you and all the people in your house."

ACTS 16:23, 25-26, 29-31

## Safe and Sound

*E*ven though they were grown men, Paul and Silas had to be scared. They had been thrown into prison. They didn't know what would happen next. But they did know one thing: God was in control. So what did they do? They sang songs—right in the middle of the jail. Next thing they knew, a big earthquake shook the prison doors open. God had rescued them and saved the jailor, too!

*W*hat scares you? Is it thunderstorms? Is it leaving mom to go to school? Whenever you feel afraid, remember the story of Paul and Silas. God is just as close to you as he was to them.

Look at the song on the following page, or choose your own favorite song. Then sing it out loud to the Lord. It will remind you that you are safe in Jesus, and it will be a beautiful sound to God!

*Adore*

# What a Friend We Have in Jesus

JOSEPH SCRIVEN

What a friend we have in Jesus,
All our sins and griefs to bear!
What a privilege to carry
Ev'rything to God in prayer!
O what peace we often forfeit,
O what needless pain we bear,
All because we do not carry
Ev'rything to God in prayer.

We know that in everything God works for the good of those who love him. They are the people God called, because that was his plan. God knew them before he made the world. And God chose them to be like his Son. Then Jesus would be the first-born of many brothers. God planned for them to be like his Son. And those he planned to be like his Son, he also called. And those he called, he also made right with him. And those he made right, he also glorified.

So what should we say about this? If God is for us, then no one can defeat us.

ROMANS 8:28-31

258

## A Good Ending

God writes the best stories. They have the happiest endings. Did you know that you have a part in God's great story about the world?

It goes like this: Before God ever made the world, he knew all about you. He planned when you'd be born and what you'd be like. At just the right time, you were born. As you live your life, it might look like nothing special is happening.

You sleep, eat, play, and enjoy life. But God is busy at work, helping you to become the special person he made you to be. He is training you for your role in helping his kingdom grow. In the end, we will live in heaven with him. We will know the full story and be amazed at how God made everything work together perfectly.

How is your day going? Does it seem like good or bad things are happening? Draw a colorful picture to celebrate a good day or to cheer yourself up if it has been a not-so-fun day. Remember that God uses everything that happens in our lives for our good, and for his good ending!

Yes, God's riches are very great! God's wisdom and knowledge have no end! No one can explain the things God decides. No one can understand God's ways. As the Scripture says,

"Who has known the mind of the Lord? Who has been able to give the Lord advice?"

...Yes, God made all things. And everything continues through God and for God. To God be the glory forever! Amen.

So brothers, since God has shown us great mercy, I beg you to offer your lives as a living sacrifice to him. Your offering must be only for God and pleasing to him. This is the spiritual way for you to worship.

ROMANS 11:33-34, 36; 12:1

## Body Language

Have you ever been to big church with your parents? First you sing music to God. Next, you pass the offering plate. And last, the pastor reads from the Bible and talks (for what may seem like a long time) about God and his Word. So which part of the service is worship to God, and which part is just "normal" church?

All of it is worship! And true worship doesn't just happen during church services, either. God says that every single moment of our lives is a chance to worship him. What do you think about when you're alone? How do you spend your time? How do you treat your parents and siblings? God wants us to use every breath we breathe to bring him glory. So you want to give God praise? Then say it, sing it, think it, serve it, and do it all for him!

*Adore*

## Activity

Make a list of the ways you can praise God. Use your crayons or colored pencils to draw pictures showing the ways you praise! After you've decorated your list, hang it on the 'frig to remind you to praise the Lord every day.

You know that in a race all the runners run. But only one gets the prize. So run like that. Run to win! All those who compete in the games use strict training. They do this so that they can win a crown. That crown is an earthly thing that lasts only a short time. But our crown will continue forever. So I do not run without a goal. I fight like a boxer who is hitting something — not just the air. It is my own body that I hit. I make it my slave. I do this so that I myself will not be rejected after I have preached to others.

1 CORINTHIANS 9:24-27

*Training your body helps you
in some ways, but serving God helps you
in every way. Serving God brings you
blessings in this life and in
the future life, too.*

1 TIMOTHY 4:8

## Fit for a Princess

**Beauty Secrets** Don't get con-fused. Kings and queens do sit on thrones. But that's not all they do. They get up. They work. And they exercise their bodies and minds to be the best rulers they can be.

God wants us to exercise, too. It's great for our bodies, and it helps us to grow strong so we can do God's work. But he also wants us to exercise our minds and hearts. We need to take time to read God's Word and pray so our spirits will grow strong in his truth. With strong muscles and hearts, we are ready to do the work God has called us to do as his royal children.

*Beauty*

*Beauty Tips*

Instead of watching TV today, think of an outdoor activity you enjoy. Maybe it's riding your bike, playing hopscotch, or jumping rope with your friends. As you play and exercise outside, ask God to strengthen your love for him, too.

I may speak in different languages of men or even angels. But if I do not have love, then I am only a noisy bell or a ringing cymbal. I may have the gift of prophecy; I may understand all the secret things of God and all knowledge; and I may have faith so great that I can move mountains. But even with all these things, if I do not have love, then I am nothing. I may give everything I have to feed the poor. . . . But I gain nothing by doing these things if I do not have love.

1 CORINTHIANS 13:1-3

# Love from Above

You could have all the money in the world. Be the smartest girl anyone's ever known. Look more beautiful than a queen. Run faster than an Olympic athlete. Have more personality than a movie star.

But God's Word says that if you don't have love, you don't have anything.

271

Nothing in this world is more beautiful than a loving heart. So how can God's princesses get this treasure? It comes from our King. As we learn to believe how much Jesus loves us, it changes our hearts, too. We begin to love others in the same wonderful way.

Truths

# Make It Yours

*W*hat is love, anyway? God gives us a good picture in the rest of 1 Corinthians 13. Have your mom read to you how God describes true love. Then have her read it again, this time putting your name in each place where it says the word "love."

Do you show that kind of love to others? Take time to pray with your mom. Ask Jesus to help both of you grow in God's kind of love.

Be careful. Continue strong in the faith. Have courage, and be strong. Do everything in love. . . .

The churches in the country of Asia send greetings to you. Aquila and Priscilla greet you in the Lord. Also the church that meets in their house greets you. All the brothers here send greetings. Give each other a holy kiss when you meet.

I am Paul, and I am writing this greeting with my own hand.

If anyone does not love the Lord, then let him be separated from God—lost forever!

Come, O Lord!

The grace of the Lord Jesus be with you.

My love be with all of you in Christ Jesus.

1 CORINTHIANS 16:13-14, 19-24

# Eye to Eye

**Princess Charming**

You're on the computer playing your favorite game. Suddenly, you hear your parents talking behind you with some visitors who have come to the house. They say they want to introduce you to their friends. Do you:

**A** Keep looking at the computer screen and say, "Hi!"

**B** Tell them to wait just a minute until you are finished.

**C** Turn around quickly, wave a hand, and then return to your game.

**D** Stop what you are doing, stand up, and greet the visitors with a smile.

As a princess, you must learn how to give a royal welcome. Whenever you meet someone new, don't be shy. Look at them in the eyes, and greet them with a smile. When you stop what you are doing to notice someone else, it shows them that you think they are important. It also helps you to remember that TV shows and games are not as important as real people. As children of the King, we need to be ready at all times to share God's love with the people he brings into our lives.

I begged the Lord three times to take this problem away from me. But the Lord said to me, "My grace is enough for you. When you are weak, then my power is made perfect in you." So I am very happy to brag about my weaknesses. Then Christ's power can live in me. So I am happy when I have weaknesses, insults, hard times, sufferings, and all kinds of troubles. All these things are for Christ. And I am happy, because when I am weak, then I am truly strong.

2 CORINTHIANS 12:8-10

# God's Great Strength

Do you remember hearing stories about when you were a little baby? Your mom had to feed you and dress you. She did everything for you. But now that you've grown older, you can do many things by yourself. Learning to take care of yourself is a normal part of growing up.

In God's family, growing up happens a little differently. The older we grow in Jesus, the more we understand how much we need his help. God knows that we are all weak and helpless without him. We must always ask him for strength and wisdom to live good lives. Only God can make us become more like Jesus. We are strongest when we trust him alone to meet our needs.

Hero

$\mathscr{A}$sk Jesus today to help you be strong for him. Remember that God gives you the power to do everything you need to do for his glory.

Praise be to the God and Father of our Lord Jesus Christ. In Christ, God has given us every spiritual blessing in heaven. In Christ, he chose us before the world was made. In his love he chose us to be his holy people—people without blame before him. And before the world was made, God decided to make us his own children through Jesus Christ. That was what he wanted and what pleased him. This brings praise to God because of his wonderful grace. God gave that grace to us freely, in Christ, the One he loves. . . .

In Christ we were chosen to be God's people. God had already chosen us to be his people, because that is what he wanted. And God is the One who makes everything agree with what he decides and wants.

EPHESIANS 1:3-6, 11

## Adopted and Adored

**My Hero**

When you are hungry, who do you ask for food? If someone hurts your feelings, who can help you feel better? Families are one of God's biggest blessings to us. We can always talk to mom or dad because we know they love us. They want to take care of us. We feel safe when we are home.

God gives us families so we can understand how God feels about us. He says that everyone who trusts in Jesus to save them has become a part of his family.

We aren't strangers or even servants. We are his precious children! He has adopted us and made us his very own. We can always feel protected and safe when we go to our heavenly Father for help. He loves us even more than our earthly parents do. What a blessing to be a part of God's family and a princess in his kingdom!

*Hero*

Children, obey your parents the way the Lord wants. This is the right thing to do. The command says, "Honor your father and mother." This is the first command that has a promise with it. The promise is: "Then everything will be well with you, and you will have a long life on the earth."

Fathers, do not make your children angry, but raise them with the training and teaching of the Lord.

EPHESIANS 6:1-4

# The Reason They Rule

It hardly seems fair—being a princess and all. You want to do the things that are fun. All play and no work sounds good to you. Why should God's girls be busy doing what someone else says to do anyway?

*Down In My Heart*

*Memory Portion:*

Children, obey your parents the way the Lord wants. This is the right thing to do.

EPHESIANS 6:1

Even princesses need to learn the ways of royalty. God picked out your parents just for you so that you can learn his ways from them. They protect you, love you, and help lead you to God. So trust that God's ways are best—even when it doesn't look like as much fun as what you had in mind. It's the right thing to do, and it leads to a closer friendship with God and your parents.

*Heart*

# Trust and Obey

JOHN H. SAMMIS AND DANIEL B. TOWNER

When we walk with the Lord
In the light of His Word,
What a glory He sheds on our way!
While we do His good will,
He abides with us still,
And with all who will trust and obey.

Trust and obey, for there's no other way
To be happy in Jesus, but to trust
and obey.

Does your life in Christ give you strength? Does his love comfort you? Do we share together in the Spirit? Do you have mercy and kindness? If so, make me very happy by having the same thoughts, sharing the same love, and having one mind and purpose. When you do things, do not let selfishness or pride be your guide. Be humble and give more honor to others than to yourselves. Do not be interested only in your own life, but be interested in the lives of others.

PHILIPPIANS 2:1-4

## A Sweet Treat

**Worthy of Love**

Jesus' followers wanted to know. What matters most to God? Jesus' answer was simple. Love God with everything you have in you, and love your neighbor like you love yourself.

So who are the neighbors Jesus is talking about? He means anybody that you meet, or anyone that you know. Jesus wants us to love everyone that he brings into our lives.

*H*e also means your real
neighbors—the people who
live beside you on your
street. God planned for
your family to live right
where you do. He also planned for your
neighbors to be there, too.
Your own neighborhood
is a great place to begin
sharing Jesus' love
with others.

*Love*

Ask your mom if you can bake some cookies for the neighbors today. Ask her to help you make some cards that let them know you and God love them. Then walk over to their door and hand them out. It's a sweet way to help share God's love and build friendships at the same time!

In your lives you must think and act like Christ Jesus. . . .

Be full of joy in the Lord always. I will say again, be full of joy.

Let all men see that you are gentle and kind. The Lord is coming soon. Do not worry about anything. But pray and ask God for everything you need. And when you pray, always give thanks. And God's peace will keep your hearts and minds in Christ Jesus. The peace that God gives is so great that we cannot understand it.

Brothers, continue to think about the things that are good and worthy of praise. Think about the things that are true and honorable and right and pure and beautiful and respected.

PHILIPPIANS 2:5; 4:4-8

*Do not be shaped by this world.*
*Instead be changed within by a new way*
*of thinking. Then you will be able to*
*decide what God wants for you.*
*And you will be able to know what*
*is good and pleasing to God*
*and what is perfect.*

ROMANS 12:2

## Beyond Hair to Beautiful Thoughts

**Beauty Secrets**

It's the time that many little princesses dread. Your mom needs to brush the tangles out of your hair. "Do you have to?" you may plead. But mom knows that if you want a beautiful head of hair, it's going to take some work.

God wants you to have a beautiful head, too. But he isn't talking about your hair. He cares about what goes on inside your head. He wants you to think like God thinks. Just like brushing tangles, changing our thoughts is hard work. When you notice you are thinking bad thoughts or thoughts that aren't true, ask God to forgive you. Ask him for wisdom. He will change your mind. He will help you think like a daughter of the King.

Beauty

# Beauty Tips

When it is time to have your hair brushed, begin a new game with your mom. Each time you feel a painful tug, remember to turn your thoughts to Jesus. As she brushes, ask God to help change your mind so that you always think like him.

Do everything without complaining or arguing. Then you will be innocent and without anything wrong in you. You will be God's children without fault. But you are living with crooked and mean people all around you. Among them you shine like stars in the dark world. You offer to them the teaching that gives life. So when Christ comes again, I can be happy because my work was not wasted. I ran in the race and won.

PHILIPPIANS 2:14-16

# Attitude Alert

*As* a princess, you have lots to do throughout your day. Some things to do are fun, some things not so fun. Whether fun or not, God's Word rules out certain activities: no complaining or arguing.

*Memory Portion:*

Do everything without complaining or arguing.

PHILIPPIANS 2:14

299

Why do you think God wants his girls to have thankful hearts? Our High King knows we are happiest when we think about how wonderful he is to us. When we complain or argue, it shows that we don't like what God has given us. It also shows that we want to serve ourselves more than God or others. But we will begin to say words of thanks when we under- stand in our hearts how good God is to his people.

Heart

# *Activity*

Have you ever gotten into trouble for complaining? What do you complain about the most? Now think of 5 things that you are most thankful for that God has given you. Color a picture of each blessing on a piece of paper, and put it by your bed. Before you go to sleep and when you wake up, remember to look at the picture and thank God for the good things in your life!

God has chosen you and made you his holy people. He loves you. So always do these things: Show mercy to others; be kind, humble, gentle, and patient. Do not be angry with each other, but forgive each other. If someone does wrong to you, then forgive him. Forgive each other because the Lord forgave you. Do all these things; but most important, love each other. Love is what holds you all together in perfect unity.... Everything you say and everything you do should all be done for Jesus your Lord. And in all you do, give thanks to God the Father through Jesus....

Be wise in the way you act with people who are not believers. Use your time in the best way you can. When you talk, you should always be kind and wise. Then you will be able to answer everyone in the way you should.

COLOSSIANS 3:12-14, 17; 4:5-6

# Open-Door Policy

**Princess Charming**

You are walking into a restaurant at the same time as another family. You should:

A Walk faster to get ahead of them in line.

B Squeeze through the door at the same time.

C Stand there and stare at them.

D Open the door for them to pass through.

If you're really hungry, it might be extra hard. But if you want to act like the princess you are, your good manners should come first. To hold the door open for someone else lets them know you think they are important. It helps you learn how to serve others, as well as grow in patience. But don't worry. Your family will be seated and eating in no time, too.

We ask you, brothers, to warn those who do not work. Encourage the people who are afraid. Help those who are weak. Be patient with every person. Be sure that no one pays back wrong for wrong. But always try to do what is good for each other and for all people.

Always be happy. Never stop praying. Give thanks whatever happens. That is what God wants for you in Christ Jesus....

We pray that God himself, the God of peace, will make you pure, belonging only to him. We pray that your whole self—spirit, soul, and body—will be kept safe and be without wrong when our Lord Jesus Christ comes. The One who calls you will do that for you. You can trust him.

1 THESSALONIANS 5:14-18, 23-24

## A Royal To-Do

**Worthy of Love**

Encourage others. Help the weak. Forgive each other. Always be happy. Always pray. Stay away from evil. Stay pure. Just hearing the list can make you tired. How can God expect so much from his little princesses? After all, you are just a kid. Shouldn't you just go out and play and get to the list a little later in life? Jesus wants your whole heart. He doesn't want it later; he wants it now. He knows that the very best life happens for his people when we obey.

*B*ut how? How can we possibly do it all now, or even later when we grow bigger?

God shares the secret in verse 24: "The One who calls you will do that for you. You can trust him." God is at work in your heart right now. He is changing you by his Holy Spirit.

*Love*

He promises that he will finish the work he has begun in you. You just need to trust your heavenly King. When you see that you are loving others and obeying God, you know that it is Jesus who is doing it through you. Then give him thanks for always keeping his promises!

Timothy, you are like a son to me. I am giving you a command that agrees with the prophecies that were given about you in the past. I tell you this so that you can follow those prophecies and fight the good fight of faith. Continue to have faith and do what you know is right. Some people have not done this. Their faith has been destroyed....

First, I tell you to pray for all people. Ask God for the things people need, and be thankful to him. You should pray for kings and for all who have authority. Pray for the leaders so that we can have quiet and peaceful lives—lives full of worship and respect for God. This is good, and it pleases God our Savior.

1 TIMOTHY 1:18-19; 2:1-3

# Teacher Talk

**Worthy of Love**

It wasn't an accident. God gave you your teacher on purpose. He put you in that class so that he could teach you through your teacher. Whether you know it or not, your teacher is a big blessing from God.

Have you ever thought that you could be a blessing to your teacher, too? God's Word tells us we need to remember our leaders.

We need to be thankful for them and pray for God to lead and protect them. When our teachers, parents, and leaders are following God, it makes it easier to follow their lead!

Today let your teacher know how much he or she means to you. At the right time, go to her desk, and ask her how she is doing. Then ask her if she has any prayer requests. Take a moment to pray for her needs right then.

*Love*

*I*f there isn't any time, you can pray at your seat or when you get home. At the end of the week, check back with her to see if her prayer requests have been answered. Even grown-ups need to know they are special!

It was by faith Abraham obeyed God's call to go to another place that God promised to give him. He left his own country, not knowing where he was to go. It was by faith that he lived in the country God promised to give him. He lived there like a visitor who did not belong. He lived in tents with Isaac and Jacob, who had received that same promise from God. Abraham was waiting for the city that has real foundations—the city planned and built by God.

He was too old to have children, and Sarah was not able to have children. It was by faith that Abraham was made able to become a father. Abraham trusted God to do what he had promised. This man was so old that he was almost dead. But from him came as many descendants as there are stars in the sky. They are as many as the grains of sand on the seashore that cannot be counted.

HEBREWS 11:8-12

## Facts of Faith

**Royal Truths**

If your mom said that she was taking you to the zoo, would you believe her? What if you didn't leave right away? What if she had lots of errands to run before it was time? Even though it is hard to wait, you would. You believe your mom and know that if she says something good is coming, then it is.

God is even more trustworthy than your mom. He says that something good is coming. He says we will one day be made perfect.

315

We will not be sick or tired anymore. We won't sin anymore. And we'll get to live with him in heaven.

Can you see heaven right now? How do you know God is telling the truth? We know God can't lie. We believe what he says. Our belief is called "faith." Faith is trusting that God will do what he promises, even if we have to wait on his timing.

Truths

Do you have faith that everything God says in his Word is true? Are you sometimes afraid that it isn't? Don't worry! God is even able to help us when we don't believe him. Just be honest. Tell God what you are thinking. Then ask him to give you the gift of faith in him. He is able to change your heart and help you hope in him.

My dear brothers, do not be fooled about this. Every good action and every perfect gift is from God. These good gifts come down from the Creator of the sun, moon, and stars. God does not change like their shifting shadows. God decided to give us life through the word of truth. He wanted us to be the most important of all the things he made.

JAMES 1:16-18

## No Shadow of Doubt

Your room is dark. Right now, you're supposed to be a sleeping princess. But the trees outside your window are moving. Long shadows sway on the walls. It might seem a little scary.

Feeling scared when we aren't sure what is going on is perfectly normal. But we have a heavenly Father who knows all things and wants the very best for us. Even when we're scared, we need to believe God.

$\mathcal{L}$ook again at the shadows. Then remember what God says about them. He tells us that though his creation changes and moves all the time, God doesn't. He always stays the same. We can count on him to always be good, always be in control, and always love us.

*Hero*

God is the only One we can always trust to not let us down. Thank him now for being the same yesterday, today, and forever. Now get some sleep!

My dear brothers, always be willing to listen and slow to speak. Do not become angry easily. Anger will not help you live a good life as God wants. So put out of your life every evil thing and every kind of wrong you do. Don't be proud but accept God's teaching that is planted in your hearts. This teaching can save your souls.

Do what God's teaching says; do not just listen and do nothing. When you only sit and listen, you are fooling yourselves. A person who hears God's teaching and does nothing is like a man looking in a mirror. He sees his face, then goes away and quickly forgets what he looked like. But the truly happy person is the one who carefully studies God's perfect law that makes people free. He continues to study it. He listens to God's teaching and does not forget what he heard. Then he obeys what God's teaching says. When he does this, it makes him happy.

JAMES 1:19-25

# First Things First

**Princess Charming**

You have had a fabulous day at school and can't wait to tell your mom about it. The problem is that your sister did, too. So you both start talking at the same time. Should you:

A. Tell your sister to be quiet so you can talk.

B. Talk really loudly so your mom will hear your story over hers.

C. Let your sister go first, and listen to what she has to say.

D. Decide you are going to pout and not tell anyone what happened.

Have you ever heard the saying, "patience is a virtue"? It is actually a fruit of the Holy Spirit — a sign that God lives in your heart. Even though it is very hard to let others speak first before us, our patience pleases God. It also gives us a chance to hear what is happening in other people's hearts and lives. Then, at the right time, you should feel free to share what is on your mind. Your thoughts are important, too!

Is there anyone among you who is truly wise and understanding? Then he should show his wisdom by living right. He should do good things without being proud. A wise person does not brag. But if you are selfish and have bitter jealousy in your hearts, you have no reason to brag. Your bragging is a lie that hides the truth. That kind of "wisdom" does not come from God. That "wisdom" comes from the world. It is not spiritual. It is from the devil.... But the wisdom that comes from God is like this: First, it is pure. Then it is also peaceful, gentle, and easy to please. This wisdom is always ready to help those who are troubled and to do good for others. This wisdom is always fair and honest. When people work for peace in a peaceful way, they receive the good result of their right-living.

JAMES 3:13-15, 17-18

# Fairest of Them All

Was it just Snow White's beauty that made her so wonderful? Was it Cinderella's dress that made her a princess? Even the fairytale princesses show the truth. They were different from the others because they had beautiful hearts. They cared just as much for the needs of others as they did for themselves.

God wants to crown his princesses with the same kind of beauty. He loves for us to be fair to everyone and unselfish in our actions.

*H*ow? We will treat others fairly when we understand how important people are to God. Their thoughts, feelings, and lives matter to God just as much as ours do. When you are tempted to demand your own way, remember this royal truth: Other people matter, too. We get even greater joy when we treat others with the fairness and respect that they deserve.

## Make It Yours

Wisdom that comes from God is always fair and honest. When we ask for God's wisdom, we'll always be ready to help others and do good things for them. Life won't always be fair. Your siblings might get something you don't. You might not get praised for every good thing you do. But God sees your heart. Trust him to look out for you while you help others.

If we say that we have no sin, we are fooling ourselves, and the truth is not in us. But if we confess our sins, he will forgive our sins. We can trust God. He does what is right. He will make us clean from all the wrongs we have done....

My dear children, I write this letter to you so that you will not sin. But if anyone does sin, we have Jesus Christ to help us. He is the Righteous One. He defends us before God the Father. Jesus died in our place to take away our sins. And Jesus is the way that all people can have their sins taken away, too.

1 JOHN 1:8-9; 2:1-2

*1 John*

# Coming Clean

**Down In My Heart**

*H*ow do you know when you are dirty and need a bath? Brown smudges on your face and hands give you a good clue. Maybe even the smell alone lets you know it's time for some soap.

## Memory Portion:

Jesus died in our place to take away our sins. And Jesus is the way that all people can have their sins taken away, too.

1 JOHN 2:2

So how can you tell when your heart is not clean? Jesus says that when we disobey him, our sin makes us dirty on the inside. Soap and water can't clean there, but God can. As soon as you know you have messed up, run to Jesus. Ask him to forgive you for choosing your way over God's way. Then ask him to help you obey the next time. He loves to make your heart as clean and white as newly fallen snow.

*Heart*

# Activity

Ask your mom if you can help her polish her silver or jewelry. Do you see how brown it is? Now wipe it with the special soap and rinse in water. Is it all bright and shiny? Remember that God cleans your heart even better than the best soap around!

This is the teaching you have heard from the beginning: We must love each other. . . .

We know that we have left death and have come into life. We know this because we love our brothers in Christ. . . . This is how we know what real love is: Jesus gave his life for us. So we should give our lives for our brothers. . . . My children, our love should not be only words and talk. Our love must be true love. And we should show that love by what we do.

1 JOHN 3:11, 14, 16, 18

## Love Letters

### Worthy of Love

How can you tell who belongs to Jesus? It's not by how good they act. It's not by how often they go to church. It's not even how much they talk about God. Jesus says that we can tell who is a Christian by how they love. Why? Because real love comes from God. You have to have God's Spirit inside your heart to be able to love others the way God does.

sk God today to fill you with his love for him and others. Then look for fun ways to share your love, beginning with your parents. Think of some reasons why you love your mom and dad.

*Love*

*T*hen color a picture for each idea that shows how you feel. Seal it up in an envelope, and put it in a special place that you know your mom and dad will find by surprise. Love is the sweetest treasure a princess can give.